*The Meaning of Things*

Also by Elaine Randell

Songs of Hesperus
Telegrams from the Midnight Country
Untitled
Seven Poems
A Taper to the Outward Roome
Early in My Life
Long Hair for Birds
This, Our Frailty
Larger Breath of All Things
Hard to Place
Songs for the Sleepless
Beyond All Other: Poems 1970–1986
Prospect into Breath
Gut Reaction
Selected Poems 1970–2005
Faulty Mothering

Elaine Randell

*The Meaning of Things*

Shearsman Books

First published in the United Kingdom in 2017 by
Shearsman Books
50 Westons Hill Drive
Emersons Green
BRISTOL
BS16 7DF

Shearsman Books Ltd Registered Office
30–31 St. James Place, Mangotsfield, Bristol BS16 9JB
*(this address not for correspondence)*

www.shearsman.com

ISBN 978-1-84861-514-4

Copyright © Elaine Randell, 2017.
The right of Elaine Randell to be identified as the author
of this work has been asserted by her in accordance with the
Copyrights, Designs and Patents Act of 1988.
All rights reserved.

ACKNOWLEDGEMENTS
'Against the Air' previously appeared in *The Star You Steer By—
Basil Bunting & British Modernism*, edited by James McGonigal
and Richard Price (Amsterdam & Atlanta, GA: Rodopi 2000).

# Contents

## I
| | |
|---|---|
| Day's work | 11 |
| Day Centre | 12 |
| Air | 13 |
| Hard to Place | 14 |
| On the Street | 22 |
| Punch Your Lights Out | 23 |
| We're lucky really | 24 |

## II
| | |
|---|---|
| Poems insist | 27 |
| Against the Air | 28 |
| Advise Yourself | 29 |
| Field | 31 |
| After Dusk | 32 |
| An Old Person Says Goodbye | 33 |
| Before I Go or the Gap Left After Leaving | 34 |
| Bulletins from Corrèze – 1989 | 35 |
| Commune Rurale – Saint-Agnan France, July 1991 | 37 |
| Courage was Cast About Her Like a Dress | 38 |
| Easter 2014 Romney Marsh | 39 |
| For Barry at 68 – July 18th 2014 | 40 |
| Forest Poems | 42 |
| In Time | 43 |
| On the Birth of Ada | 44 |
| Parents | 45 |
| Peeling Quail's Eggs: At 60 | 46 |
| Suppose the Unpredictable Wave Was God | 47 |
| The Body is Still the Measure of All Things | 48 |
| The Flower Has Spent Its Energy and Has Gone to Seed | 49 |
| And Therefore Was Her Labour That Much More in Washing and Wringing | 52 |
| The Light That Is | 53 |
| The Meaning of Things | 54 |
| What Would This Day Want from Us | 60 |

| | |
|---|---:|
| For LH at Brighton Station | 61 |
| From the Window | 62 |
| After Dusk | 63 |
| To be Loved Is to Be Noticed | 64 |
| To Love Is to Notice | 64 |
| Note Love | 65 |
| To Notice Is to Love | 65 |
| Try to See This Then | 66 |
| News – One: Gulf Crisis | 67 |
| It's Easier Now | 68 |

## III

| | |
|---|---:|
| Court in Progress | 73 |
| In the Village | 75 |
| Luxury Goods | 77 |
| Queuing | 78 |
| Sharply Across the Top of the Head | 79 |
| That's How | 80 |
| Without Blinking | 81 |
| Which We Weren't | 82 |
| Achilles Heel | 83 |
| Easter Holiday London Trip | 85 |
| What She Said | 86 |
| In Her Caravan | 87 |
| My Dad | 87 |
| Danny | 88 |
| Susan | 88 |
| When He Asked Her | 89 |
| Neighbours | 97 |
| Notes Towards Loss | 99 |
| Stories from the Contact Centre | 101 |
| Stunned by the Misery | 112 |
| The Seat | 116 |

## IV

| | |
|---|---:|
| My Mother, Part 1 | 121 |
| My Father, Part 1 | 128 |

*Dedicated to my parents,*
*Daphne Pauline Randell*
*12.2.1927–20.9.2005*

*Henry William Randell*
*8.5.1919–12.2.1979*

1

# Day's work

Face

Turning to me he says
that Father Christmas had not known what they had wanted
                         so he hadn't come that day but still
it had been the best day of his life
The boy looks at me for a long time studying me
he says he knows why I have come today
"It's about the baby,
he's cute" he says
The boy's long white thin arms are like glass
His face his face his face is totally opened to me
Is the baby dead now he asks
I tell him so

## Day Centre

In the damp condemned Methodist Church hall
I visit Susan.
Her varicose legs in bobby socks
fold under the broken chair
as we speak of her children
now 6 and 9 she has not seen for
two years.
Susan's
16-year-old boyfriend cuddles her
calls her Mum.
Above us on the wall there is Jesus
in a faded print
"suffer the little children".
We wait outside together
passing the font, the hymn books are
under dust sheets. The nurse calls them
back for their 'medication' time.
Susan grabs my arm,
"You will tell them won't you
that I'm marrying Pete." She
nuzzles his neck.
"Only I want the boys to
make me a card."
O abnormal lunatic giant of the world
I stand with life explained.

# Air

I was there
Just by it
When it happened. He said to look away and he shouted but I didn't. It sort of compels you doesn't it when someone says don't look. I wasn't the same after that.
It probably took only seconds and I could hear mum's voice in my head that tea was on the table. Odd isn't it, the things that go through your mind. I remember the edge of his trouser leg that's all I could see. The noise reminded me of air going out of balloon like the day when Sonia had the party and dad couldn't tie the ends up and she laughed a lot. Only she didn't laugh when it happened. She was still, very still and dead quiet. Dead dead quiet and very still. I shan't forget how still she was. Years later I've thought of that.
When the police asked me what I saw I told about his trouser leg and me being on the top bunk all the time and him knowing that.

# Hard to Place

*'Hard to Place was written while working for "Children need Families a project of the Children's Society which places children with special needs into adoptive families.*

I
His mother, a petrol pump attendant, was said
by those who knew her to be far less than bright.
She had not wanted the child but had wanted his
father. She grew very fat with the pregnancy
but told no one of the forthcoming child inside
her. On the forecourt of the garage she went
into labour while delivering three gallons of
four star. They stifled screams with the
rag that wiped the dip stick and mopped her waters
with the sponge that cleaned the windscreens.

Now eight years later he's a tiny child and the
doctors write notes about his tiny head
circumference and his stammer. He has moved foster homes
eight times in the last three years. He is a
difficult boy. The woman from the children's home writes
on his review form that he's a nice enough child
but that he often uses situations to his own
advantage. His gait is odd, she comments, and
he frequently limps to attract the attention of
adults.

II
It must have been an odd thing from the start.
The way they had met, the differing backgrounds
from where they both came. He was from a strong
Jewish family, his father had been murdered by the
Nazis, his mother was said to be beautiful but no

one could recollect what became of her. It is
known that he was proud of his Jewish heritage and
that he played the violin. He was nineteen years old
when he met the girl who later became his wife.
She was a farmer's daughter who developed an addiction
to heroin; later she became a prostitute. There is
a photograph of her on the file wearing a tiny black mini
skirt and holding one of her sons in her arms; her face is
tear stained. A few days later she
killed herself.

The two sons have no living memory of her, they have,
throughout their lives met their father on three
occasions but the interviews were brief and his
whereabouts are unknown.

The boys don't form relationships very easily and
they tend to test adults out to see how far they
will go before they snap. They rarely smile and
say they want to live in a family where someone can
teach them to play the violin.

III
After her brother had been killed by swallowing
bleach she came into care. Her mother had
asked that she be taken away before she harmed
her. The last she saw of her mother was never
to be forgotten, she has no recollection of her
father at all but it is believed he works on a
fairground. She frequently has terrible nightmares
that wake the whole home. The staff say she
encourages the boys to come into her room. She has
absconded on two occasions when the Fair has been
in town.

Her mother is now in prison and she had written
to her but received no reply.

The staff at the home would like her to live
in a family to be taught some discipline since
everyone believes she is promiscuous and could
be in moral danger. She is nine years old and
calls her dolly 'Mummy'.

IV
It is noted that at the age of four years
he possesses a very full and foul vocabulary.
His toenails were broken and bleeding caused
by his walking with his toes curled under. He
is a very anxious and tense little boy. It
is rare for him to show affection but he is
keen to please. His birth occurred an
hour after his father had kicked his mother
and subsequently he was three months premature.
She is now an agoraphobic, quiet, sullen with
bleached hair; she has the appearance of a
clown. It would seem that she cannot read and
did not attend school from the age of twelve.
The boy's father has toes missing from his left
foot due to an accident at work; he has a sister
who is blind. He was a baker who became a miner.
It is fair to say that neither parent wishes
to have care of the child but both will fight
through the courts.

His foster parents say that he is most unsettled
and appears to be worried. He has pulled out
handfuls of his hair but he is an attractive
boy who will respond to constancy.

V
The first meeting the couple had with the child
they hoped they would learn to love was brief
and during their stay they were told how wearing
he could be and how he pestered for new activities
every few minutes. At this meeting he kissed and
cuddled them both and as they said goodbye he
refused to watch their car draw away.

At the second meeting they took him out alone to
a café and he told the waitress that she was
beautiful. They took him to the seaside and he
jumped into the ocean fully clothed.

When they took him home for a weekend he sat up
all night and picked the stuffing from his mattress.
The next day he was taken to the Dreamland amusement arcade
and rode on the dodgems; he ate ten Bounty bars and
was not sick. Later in the afternoon he pulled the
chandelier from the ceiling and threw the standard
lamp across the room, he kicked all the chairs and
dented the washing machine. He told the couple
that he loved them and could not face life alone in
a children's home. Their efforts to control him
failed, their efforts to love him collapsed.
At the next visit they told him he was
too much for them. They were distressed and disappointed.
"Who will take me to Dreamland now?" he said just
before he was driven away.

VI
"Sometimes he holds on to me so tightly at
night I fear his heart will burst."
The infant is three years old and suffers
from Down's Syndrome. He is a strong happy

boy whose eyes can barely focus. He is
partially sighted.

At the hospital after the delivery was over
his mother was heard to continually shout
"Don't let me take that monster home, don't
make me, don't make me." His cries were
quickly stifled from the other mothers but
they knew. His father, a large stocky
friendly man, an ironmonger's assistant, wanted
to keep the infant but later conceded to
his wife's rejection.

"Sometimes I feel the harder he holds on
to me it means the stronger he loves. No,
I rarely think about his natural parents,
only once perhaps when he was dangerously
ill and they thought his little heart would
give out—then I thought, "They don't know
about all this and the fight that's in him.
We are delighted to have adopted him, he's
our own angel."

VII
Late one January night when the whole house
was sleeping the young mother put her careful
plans into action and slipped away from her
family and its life. The three tiny children
remained asleep until 7.00 a.m. and their father
until 9.00 a.m. It has long been agreed that the
woman has returned to Ireland and all efforts
to trace her through the newspapers, police and
Salvation Army have now been terminated.

When the children realised their mother had gone
they tried to ring her on their toy telephones
and sent her letters through the Mr Men post office.
They cried themselves to sleep most nights and
became greedy for food constantly.

When their father realised his wife had gone he
spent the family allowance at the bookies and
told the welfare that something would have to
be done. He signed them into care and jumped
beneath the Northern Line train on the way home.
It is true to say that the children, who are
6, 4 and 2 years, are a handful and tend to be
clingy. Only last week the eldest boy was found
asking a policeman to please find his mummy.

VIII
Weighing only three pounds at birth there was
much concern expressed by all who knew the
circumstances. Both the child's parents had learning
difficulties and the mother had not known of her
pregnancy until the morning she woke earlier
than usual feeling rather wet between the legs
and pains in her stomach.
She was delighted to discover herself to be a mother
and those who knew her endeavoured to
help her as much as was possible. She was unaware
that babies defecated and was once found pushing
tissues into the child's mouth to stop him
vomiting.

At the court hearing to secure the infant's safety
the parents agreed they could not care for their
offspring and preferred their childless life which
was mainly nocturnal. After dark they cycled

miles together searching amongst tips for clothing and other
things that interested them.

The child has always been of a slight build and he
finds feeding difficult. He has been asking about
his parents and if he could meet them soon.

IX
It has all been rather too much one way and
another. The fact that her boyfriend had
been taken away in a police car that morning,
her phone being cut off, the flat reeked of shit and damp
then the child was fretful.

She collected together her purse, pushchair
and raincoat and set off for the shopping
precinct. Once inside she felt better but
the child moaned for sweets and the piped
music mixed with the lights and her lack of
food made her dizzy. Sitting down
next to an elderly couple who were rearranging
their shopping, she inquired whether they
would keep an eye on the child while she
found a toilet. Two hours later the couple
continued with their attempt to extract information
from the wailing child. Eventually the precinct
security guard took the child away and a police
woman was called. The sobbing of the infant
drowned even the piped music.

Now, four years later, the little girl has a new
family who worry about her insecurity and dreadful
fear of open spaces.

X
"All I know about me Dad is that he
murdered my little sister when she
was eighteen months old and I was five.
I know that he was from Glasgow and only
had one eye. My Mum came to see me just
after I came into the home but she was
very ill and they took her to a hospital
for diffy people where she still is.
I think being in the home with all the
other children was better than being
with my parents. I miss my little sister
though. I hope if you do find me a home
it won't be with diffy people, I've had
enough of them." She laughs and shakes her
head of yellow and green streaked hair.
At thirteen years she possesses the
body of a woman and the warmth and humour
of a friend. "I don't remember much about
him doing her in really, only that one
moment she was laughing because she'd
pulled his newspaper to bits and the next
she wasn't."

## On the Street

The dark bodies muddle across the road.
The men move together laughing in doorways watching the girls
their legs studded with mud
they walk as if
there is some uncertainty ahead.
The men start calling out, *Hello Slutty,* at the girls
who turn
raising ringed hands to their Winehouse beehives.
Giggling they shout back at the men
*hello tiny dicks.*
There is a scuffle and one of the girls is now on the ground with
a man above her,
the friends are squealing and laughing.
The dark bodies are tangled against the sodium lights.
One boy walks away; across his back his tee shirt says
Screw Perfection.

## Punch Your Lights Out

Across the tarmac
sick and torn up
adverts from Pinocchio Pizzas flap in the roadway.
Running heart attack    Racing stroke   Retching tumour
He didn't mean to watch
she didn't see him staring
did she
might she
did her eye turned in like that make it
possible?
Vomit on his shoe
"I'll punch your lights out" he heard that.

In class they told him
"concentrate, concentrate for God's sake for one minute will you."

## We're lucky really

She said
The large child freed himself from her lap forcing himself on
                                                       to the floor
It could be worse
I've seen them
She said
The boy's head lolled from side to side as he lifted himself up.
"Bastards, you're all bastards" he screamed
into her face lifting his heavy arm towards her shoulder.
Slowly she stroked his head
wiped the wetness from his face
handed him a Cheesy Wotsit.
Some boys can't even speak
she said.
We're lucky like that.

II

## Poems insist

to be written.

*Those kinds of poem which take place between people are ones I'm particularly drawn to.
Silences are places where poetry starts and stops, where taboo subjects wait to be touched on. If there's something that isn't able to be said, poetry might try to make it sayable, or find a way of pointing to what remains to be intuited.*

Hard to say this                                                            but
I feel you're on the edge of something.
A skylark bursts out from the field
swoops low, then, halfway up drops down.
Black reeds, Glyceria maxima line the dank dyke but
lit with sun and light wind they perform dark green sweet-grass
song and dance. St Rumwold's church leans over, heard it before.
The steady shoulders of the chalk Lymne hill, *"that chalk cliff in whose rift we lie."* Topped with its clean hair style of trees, their grade four point cut.
I remember being like you as this age.
What can I tell you that you would hear?
Don't waste this time I might say, buck up.

*Peter Robinson, *Through Frosted Glass: An Interview with Peter Robinson* by Ian Sansom, *Talk About Poetry* (Shearsman Books, 2006).

## Against the Air

The bright edge of the woodpecker steals
Across the gaunt
Limb of sky
    We are already gripped as she
    Steadies
    Leans and steers into the mossed
    Centre of what is contained, known.

A dark feathering in the undergrowth of woodland
Our tired burdens draw us
We tread without thought
    Driven by the flustered hope
    Again we are still unprepared
    And yet not asleep
    Or rested, even now.

The Northern stars are seen in the South too
Our poems are but small messages of quiet silence
Plain, empty, the air is against us as we try to make sense
    Evidenced by love of
    One to another
    The bridge edge of the woodpecker.

*November 1999*

## Advise Yourself

At the clouds of starlings
a sudden bequest as
the round, broad, elongated, flock shifts
funnelling and then thickening, thinning, spiralling, banking
on the edge, veering into and against the wind across the marsh
they fly united.


Advise yourself
about the loyalty of birds how the starlings turn the sky black
with their closeness
wheeling, turning, sinking, downward
young wings mix with the old.
This swooning aerial dance
as they locate a communal night-time shelter
reed beds and cliffs find them safety, warmth and confidence
peregrine falcons
struggle to target in the
hypnotising flocks.


Advise yourself as
starling flocks poised to tip
instantly and completely transformed, like metals magnetised
or liquid turning to gas. Each starling in a flock is connected to
the other. A starling turns when its neighbour turns operating
in proteins and neurons hinting at universal principles as yet to
be understood.


Advise yourself
quickly for there is safety in numbers.
The bees cluster and suck

driven by success and protection
glorious honey sold on roadsides by children
whose clear blue eyes scald into their devout weathered features.


Advise yourself
for there is only so much to see
by glimpsing
as we dash from our own shadow's.
Rest from competition as the sparks of the night bend from our taut bodies.

# Field

Bursting flight instant
out of
bushy cover
rattled calling
the pheasant gives his warning
into air
skimming
veering into
wet ditches but for sudden quiet
forestalling
a new
intrusion
into shrubby wetlands.

## After Dusk

Time after time someone slips away.
Just leaving the table and are gone.
No word
There was no plan that they would do this, vanish and not
return, become extinct.
Too often we lose those we love
and those who we did not love enough.
How easily the body lets go of itself, glad of the sleep.
The meal left unfinished
for others to tidy away.
Instead we set a new place, round off the edges, make it fitting.

November, the earth is cold and sodden, the trees push through soil, its long slow hard shadows, brave leaves, some gone, still a few bright golden somehow hanging on.
It doesn't matter anymore that the chair is empty in the sunshine or that the long shadows fall across the grass too early.
There was too much to do before sunset and somehow the last beam went unnoticed.

# An Old Person Says Goodbye

There is now a glazed artificiality about her
Sickness is the loneliest place on earth she says
The fear is there's no telling when it might strike
No insurance policy to guard against it
No special diet to be certain

up above
the shooting star
a gift a sudden thought flashes across
it's over
gone but
It's been good, nothing to regret she says

The cow turns     to her calf
Moans for its survival
its safety
That's all

# Before I Go, or the Gap Left After Leaving

So, what is needed?
Equipment in preparation for moving away     a logic is needed
but,
in front of that, you need the knowledge of being loved,
known for who you are. *It's belonging* that sets the course.
A ticket and a reason to move away, to branch out or to go, to die
*to leave and to meet strangers*
so then it's a heady divide; driven, determined,
de decretar, interior, heart.

The loss within            collapse            chance *what does not
change is the will to change*
all options but        anchored, we are kept from our worst
floundering by correlation, link.
Being in mind.
The sea air is bracing
the pool charms and the plants greenery cuts with a smell     a
simple device    sensory *When the coast was not the coast and sea
was a shell.*

So what to do before leaving
Packing away, tiding the unkempt and unravelled.

Since you left
there has been much to do.

# Bulletins from Corrèze—1989

At the circus in Excideuil the woman who sold us our ticket was also the woman who balanced a wooden post on her gold slippered foot; she later put the snakes around her neck while holding their heads away from her face; she didn't smile.

After, when the Ringmaster, wearing a brown everyday suit and Monoprix brown plastic casual shoes and carrying a whip, said, "Le spectacle est terminé," the woman began packing her gold slipper into a tiny space on the trailer next to her tumble drier and the snake basket.

Phoebe has learnt to skip; she asks me to watch her.
I marvel at her beauty.
She picks cowslips and dandelions and dock leaves and sings, sings "Mr Bluebird's on my back".

My Janet Reger top is a disappointment. Its brief life has fallen short of the advertiser's claims. The £17 has been wasted. Firstly it fell out of my suitcase and caught in the boot of the car before departure, leaving heavy oil stains from the boot lock. "It fell out," he said, "I didn't see it." I washed it when we got to France; it caught in the washing machine door and was torn so now it has oil stains and a tear.

At Chourgnac-d'Ans
We walked in silence while the girls collected cowslips, competing for the longest. The dogs barked at us making sure we'd gone out of sight before stopping, pleased to see a stranger to finally see off.

Beatrice eats goat's cheese from the packet; she leans on her sister.
"You're making my germs sore," said Naomi, "get off, I want to sleep." We watch her two-year-old frame struggle and kick.
Later she says,
"I feel better now, sit down," and we see her watch us from the corner of her eyes.

# Commune Rurale—Saint-Agnan France, July 1991

*for Beatrice*

In the stone church we go to the corner, we light a candle
"for a soul", I tell you.
You are six years old and remark on the light from the glass as it
        falls onto the wooden statue as it holds an infant Christ
An old woman bathes her head in the holy water.
We turn and head towards the door.
There is light across an effortless sky
Blue
Pink
We hold its
long shadows
In moments we chance to love
you dance.

## Courage Was Cast About Her Like a Dress

Whose form we lean upon
This oiled hope is loosened between our eyes
A man waved, raised his hand
Was that all?
On the parapet at Château Puyguilhem red orange ochre fields
A man leans, pauses
Spends time by the gate with a friend
Was that all?

## Easter 2014 Romney Marsh

On such a day the skylark
heard above the tractor before seen
up that high.
Who could not be charged
by his ecstatic salute to life
upwards and yet further up he shows how to sing while flying
while
plummeting
vertically effortlessly hovering before parachuting back.
On such a day you had also heard this
known perhaps that despite their aerial activities,
skylarks nest on the ground not in trees which may catch the wind.

## For Barry at 68 — July 18th 2014

Arriving that first day, face forward
occipital posterior as they say,
meeting head on    the gall
grit   while
others were having their say. Plenty of it seems. Swallowed it
                                                  whole and
as a child
          like a man
but you a child
took it on the chin
into your heart lipped with fear.
Marred
Spleen smudged with angered borrowed scenarios,
Shelley moulded your wrists into poems.
*Cradled in visions of hate and care,*
*And each one who waked as his brother slept,*
Sweet songs that spoke with ruptured frenulum
shock tactics which became real
Commotion    ordeal    thrill and gladness
It shook you up
as a child,
proper bruised you
making that cankered
tender wound, harden
getting even
as a child         assaulted
scar tissues that wreaked upon others, left you
draped over a sick bowl.
Meantime
buried distress in red boots
*The days are bright and filled with pain*
*Enclose me in your gentle rain*

clenched by Tyneside steel air.
In Allendale our forearms drenched your entire step in my
                                                        floured hands.

Still, I see you worrying the stars like a terrier,
the May mornings lost beneath the cowslips' shadow
carry you high these days.

# Forest Poems

### Stirring
Then there is the frog with his single
Thin note
Defending his territories
Until the crickets chime into the middle of things
Leading the cockerels with dogs in their unison towards the
                                                  call to prayer
Calling
The bright wanton light wakes
Swabbing the soil.


### Wedding
First there is the drumming, a gun shot and then the sound
                                        of the Zurna is close
Statice
Car horns
There is trust in planting anything, troughs, trees and promises
tortoise glide effortlessly into bright thickets.


### Cairns
A marker on the track side
Bee man at work, stream nearby, burial place, water, a warning
something to be recalled, not lost, reclaimed later.
Waymark, trail blazer
No simple stone piled on to another but deliberate passed on,
cautionary.
The cut branch, hatched tree, an old net, each bulletin
that others went before.

# In Time

*For Naomi 9 August 2008*

The sky drives us forward
as the edge of sun tilts us headlong
across the scented bay, pine forest air.
Crossing, our paths, take off as the sun climbs
hearts chasing        ants scupper
tortoises lay          stone still
bees cluster          frantic driven
in tune
as ideas are forged
our feet pound the ground
we move at the very edge of things
in time.
The earth urges us headlong
as the moon watches out for our
sleeping frames.

## On the Birth of Ada

Seagulls swoon
wheel into the light
as your head crowns into a first morning
The castle on its volcanic seat glimpses
the fine pink edges of you as the first summer morning
flower blinks into the fresh open
beauty of your face
lit
with love for there is
such abundant sky

Parents

I smell the lilacs for you
Because you couldn't
And as I did
your voice
was
just a thrush
lighting up into spring
a new blue
a glimpse and then gone
like you
just gone
like that
and yet often here
within the white
within the purple here
here with me
just
knowing and being among the
intention of you

# Peeling Quail's Eggs: At 60

These tiny gifts: stolen clutches
prying hidden
fingers age and swell
shells crack    fracture
under pressure.
My own steel grey hair now
a nest of neither wise nor foolish.
The quail's eggs with their slightest, hearts of finesse, wait their turn.
Three children now grown; I watch them.
"Therefore a hen, even when she has left her eggs, always has the
             attitude of listening with a bent ear."
When we become older
Hesitancy drags around our ears
Caution flaps and scars intent
Doubt drums on our shoes
and
yet even though we know more than the nonchalant youth
we find it
tricky to show what we already know
unable to
toss caution to the breeze and benefit bravado as easily.
The quails know something new
make the most of it and give up their eggs for pleasure

## Suppose the Unpredictable Wave Was God

We have been hoist by our own petard
that caught us out after all.
Was that just our own fear upon which so much is based,
especially love?

To feel safe the falcon faces the wind
On the whole our backs are turned.

Catkin powder
dense, cylindrical, often drooping this cluster of unisexual
apetalous flowers
willows, birches, and oaks
they stain her dress.
O brighter star with keen eye
the day so much wants to see itself in you.

# The body is still the measure of all things

and we are caught between bright mornings and heavy soil.
The vulnerable change us
we steal their goodness which stunts,
our vitriol clashes against poisoned need.
Our separate torched wisdom shrivels before the defenceless
                                                                          and exposed.
The unprotected are not weak and their strengths lifts our hearts.
We hang back ashamed by our inadequate limbs
and abandoned best.

# The Flower Has Spent its Energy and Has Gone to Seed

## Beans
Like skin of
old long dead persons
burnt bodies
scorched frames
those too tired to live any longer.
The hard nut brown content implies secure assured
A universe in hand a
believable steady prospect.


## Poppies
Random
impatient
to be gone
to spread
a colour
impetuously
never missing a chance to lend few kind colours
sudden and disinhibited enmeshed and ready.


## Tomatoes
Hidden the yellow specks slip
break out when left alone
leaving their withdrawn secret
fruit to the end.

## Candytuft
Humorous winged and ready for dispersal
their shuttlecock faces
turn to the light
letting go emblazoned
cavalier.

## Nicotiana
Understated, the miniscule
modest dance of almost spores
Shaken but firm in the idea and inkling of chance and opportunity
of future five pointed florets
the seeds leave suddenly
startling the ground.

## Aquilegia
Percussive and persuasive with swaying bucket shapes they tip
conclusive and driven
their ambition rides
on helter skelter arbitrary cloudless skies.

## Cabbage
Round and plenty
A promise of more they slip between and under
Leaving us in no doubt of their intent.

Lettuce
Eye like they blink and wide awake
Their suddenness shakes us revealing a
Frowning knotted self which folds open hearted upwards.


Nasturtium
Resolute gritted soul with fleshy promise
Seducer your wrinkled nose
rolls readily steadfast with
its thickset ample voice.


Pumpkin
Confident its opportunity remains buoyant
Potential rattles its parched
desiccated home
insulated by bulky prospects.

## And Therefore Was Her Labour
## That Much More in Washing and Wringing

To worry
is to be connected with
The woman's lot is to worry
to be troubled with          concerned, mixed up
Loaded windless the sky takes fear, returns it laundered ready.
Waiting for fortune to happen upon them
the men take chances wonder at the reeling birds diesel streets.
We are not simply *done for*
there is more to understand. The women are gathered, *"not in*
   *extravagant postures but huddled weeping, their eyes*
   *reddened and dashed with tears."*
The white daisies spring up in anticipation
they are known.
Women hem garments their hands sick with action
faces wrenched with ideas and sleepless O they are sleepless
footless, heartless hurt.
Women sweat at night
finished with swooning they know what to fear and what
                                        cannot be avoided.
Wrecked on reality some stumble on stones, heave the giant
           gems and play, toying with the needy boys.
Where are the men standing?
are they alone or in unison rowdy with lofty fear and rage?
Some become tearful expectant
stagger at a loss, tearful,
trounced others swagger on the bridge wide open and forgotten.

# The Light That Is

*for Phoebe*

Sometimes the light is so
it reaches to the bottom of the sea.
This is a sign.
hope and what we might yet get to know.
He had ruined part of this, his whole life, by worrying.
Should they have fallen
one by one like dead trees heaped up
it would stifle or smother
possibilities, a child even.

There is a fleeting second
when you
see your children no longer being yours but another's.
Lit by prospect
they dance
as you stand by
spare and quite blinded
with their awful radiance.

# The Meaning of Things

1

By the canal
Down feathers wait to be used
to line nests
or lay just lay.
The simplest of all feathers
the down touches
the heart, the whiteness the most tender
natal covering.

The sheep
eye up watching then resume grass while
hooves press Marsh down-edged dykes.

Nestlings develop their down layer within hours of hatching
body down lies under the contour feathers, the very edge
of who they are, what dependence we see.

Yolk yellow
the gorse is tucked into the armpit of the hill below the
languid cattle     necks stretched towards.

2

Look how the trees are thrust up against the window
like young girls taken against their will
bruised, their lips shake against a swollen tongue, they are not
 to be the same again.
A sense of wool between the teeth
The stone pine, *Pinus pinea*,
O so we see you Umbrella Pine gawping across the city as
hopeful tourists gobble buildings as their own.
No wonder poor Keats died in the middle of the Spanish Steps
with the cold in his bones and thoroughly disappointed like that
what with the others barging past not seeing the binds of his
chest or the caution of his heart. Ignoring his worries that he
"*may never live to trace*
*their shadows, with the magic hand of chance.*"

3

The Meaning of Things
Slips through our fingers
In winter the trees pledge a future
The clustered flower buds of
wild cherry bluntly pointed
Rowan grey with a hint of purple with dense white hairs
Elder spiked and arranged in pairs
Beech long thin spindled solitary.

The meaning of things
barely glimpsed
The birds in winter hunker down
save energy although many still sing.

4

The Meaning of
Things
a blessing in
disguise an effective
camouflage
of optimism rains on
our new shoes.
The sheep follow
watchful for a smart change in direction.


A blessing in disguise
no masquerade for this erect evergreen with its leafy stems.
Shy bowl-shaped flowers are borne in loose clusters here now in
                                        the ice packed soil
where I summon your steadying hand on my back, there at all
                                        times. Helleborus niger
St Agnes Rose Christ's herb
spread perhaps the final supper stamens silk against worn lips.


A blessing in disguise

A sense of wool between the
teeth.
Over time, the disgust is unfastened from its original fettered
horror. So, to the forest at night. Frog cricket dog cockerel of
which we are part our sleep noise joining
before the light hits the tree.

5.

The Meaning of Things
wrapped into Evensong
could it change something inside a person
an idea of
being borne aloft before the heart stops. Dead.
Mandolin wind
perhaps only the striking limbs of the fallen girl Pearl
is all that speaks
tongue tied as she was
trees line the path                             their rotted
roots letting go behind the scenes.
Those who have left us here press their seal;    it's where we are
"and above this vast open countryside rose a hot sun that soon thrust the mist back into the ground".

6.

The meaning of things can be

*The emergence of something like personality comes from the falls and tantrums and the striving.*

But don't forget the wave of chance.
A light drizzle of sun
lighting.
Buzzards circle
and their mewing across the field stays all day.
Their preoccupation with food shapes the field
small birds steer clear   rabbits flit   pheasants rattle off into
blackberry hedgerow.

We can only be loved by anyone as far as we are willing to have our own hearts broken.

# What Would This Day Want from Us

what with the heady
stretches of the south downs beyond the field
its flawless stippled prospect.
The heart's movement towards a chance that it might stop
a reminder to see the bolt blue iris
backed by Conker red beech hedge. All things in time
all things in time he said.

What would this day want from us
while silted fields lean into the canal
as Romney sheep clutter the ridge. Their whiteness herringboned
                              loose across sky largesse
as white Egrets pepper the field
their snowy whiteness plumed stark
touches the lime green field.

# For LH at Brighton Station

Both eyes closed
we hold that

just a
flash
of you walking towards the beach away from us. *The blur of
sky this white grey morning*
it quickens the spirit
and maybe only you knew the inevitability.
But it brings us here
now together as
poets
holding
holding
ourselves fast against the inevitability.

Harry's red shirt and bright eye slips into the crowd
touches his hat in greeting
I tip my umbrella
we find different trains, joint purpose.

*20th August 2015*

## From the Window

These are the days he had called his life
some were harder than others          he dragged his feet
spanning a gulf between what others seemed to enjoy, available
on offer, a special chance each week leaving him less to play
                                        with but more
short bursts of envy and regret
outside the tips of trees opened outward and up
nothing should ever be feared again
this he knew.
Honesty and renewal
this is the life he had called his days
he was having his turn
even love usually rests on dread
this he knew.

# After Dusk

Time after time someone slips away.
Just leaving the table and are gone.
No word
there was no plan that they would do this, vanish and not return,
become extinct.
Too often we lose those we love
and those who we did not love enough
How easily the body lets go of itself, glad of the sleep.
The meal left unfinished
for the others to tidy away.
Instead we set a new place, round off the edges, make it fitting.

November, the earth is cold and sodden, the trees push through soil, its long slow hard shadows, brave leaves, some gone, still a few bright golden somehow hanging on.
It no longer matters that the chair is in the sunshine or that the long shadows fall across the grass too early.
There was too much to do before sunset and somehow the last beam went unnoticed.

## To be Loved Is to Be Noticed

Seasons creep into our features.
We grow accustomed to hiding
slipping as we do over the long autumn wand
held by the eucalyptus with its red tender red blood veins.
We remark on its likeness to the wrists of children.
Spilt onto the world from our mothers' hearts,
the first taste of longing begins.

## To Love Is to Notice

Plants are sociable it's known,
their acoustic signals generate
from cell to cell
allowing rapid
communication, chatting between nearby plants.
Did you hear them?
We skirt their long gowns they gossip between themselves
spilling their seeds secretly behind their hands.

## Note Love

Presumably, many birds die in flight      their bodies drop
from the sky.
Still the magpies prolong their fight over the Liquidambar tree
marking it as their territory.
late November and the sky is folding
collapsing into rapid dusk.
Are the dead birds
devoured or
buried or
perish rotting
decaying
rapidly before we wake.

## To Notice Is to Love

How the sun runs into the room
when children are born they guide their parents towards hope
as she passed by
the faintest smell of mimosa mixed with cedar
it quite caught his arm.

## Try to See This Then

The darkness is only the light waiting
the lambs suckle unaided
bent heads of flowers
open in time
without comfort.

Try to see this then
what is remembered as the day closes down
acts of warmth
joining.

Try to see this then
at night across forest
the cockerels call out
sound leaping on the backs of the dog howling across the tracks
bees suckle, their anger bleeds into mistakes
swallows swooping lower leave too soon
the tortoises glide effortlessly into bright thickets.

# News—One
# Gulf Crisis

18.08.90

The Foreign Secretary's tie
is slightly askew.
Sir Douglas Hurd tells us
"the Military situation is prepared and ready.
I am investigating all avenues."
In Baghdad Sandy Gall looks old,
looks ill with hair too short,
tells us that people are fleeing with their
roof racks bulging, looking for homes.
King Hussein raises his papers in the air
the people praying in the mosques kick
off their plastic shoes, kneel down on
rope mats.
The American soldiers salute the USA and
hold up pictures of Uncles Ben's rice and
Big Macs. Their tanned bodies lean against
the metal tanks.
President Bush rocks comfortlessly side to side
in his golfing buggy—tells us about sanctions
and strategies. He mutters
and waves reassuringly.
The plastic shoes in the temple shuffle.

## It's Easier Now

1

What is left of my father's harvest
has lapped into the soil to bear fruit.
The birds have that look about them
I saw them thirst and suckle.
Tethered against the moss stones the tiny
violets shy away from fame.
Without the energy to form a shadow he moves
through us into laughter. The light breeze
against my foot, minute ideas chase the tip
of the afternoon. Nightingale heart.


2

Dream air. Flap away you quiet hours.
The heart is but a token of the body.
Stubbled visions and the hair runs wild
with blazing ink.
Walking like this O floss O talcum:
a bright stream of sunlight lights up your hair
but I can't say how this holds me here. Hold on
to that piece of your target. The dry weather
has made the nettles lose their sting.


3

What are the poets doing tonight?
Rounded mouths fill with petals
my arm is lost. It's only paper
on which they write. Despair

maroons. Walk on grass. Sleep on stilts
and eat water.
In the dust skulls wake up.
Look we don't love like the flowers
we haven't got it in us to be that
open.
Of exit and idea it's a wanton
access across your shoulders.


4

I try hard.
The geese in the moonlight. A bloated stiff
dead chicken drowned in sheep dip, white daisies
under my lips, my gums have cracked with effort.
All swimmers must take the plunge. It's too easy
to be still let me light up the mud.
My face is lines. A map is retrospect.
Revisions response issues we see we feel we read
we turn over a new leaf and
find no index.

III

## Court in Progress

The girl is physically large, her face is blotchy with the crying, mascara running. She glances across the court at her mother who will not look at her.

"Will you tell the court—did you notice anything strange about Kim on the Friday evening?"
"No, she was fine, she got down from the sofa herself."
"Did she eat her food?'
"No, she was picky."
"Did she sleep that night?"
"No, she was whining as usual."
"Who put her to bed?"
"Brian, he always put her to bed."
"Did anything different happen that night?'
"Yes, it was a different whingeing, high-pitched."
"What did Brian do about that?"
"He told her that if she didn't stop he'd hit her until she shone like a beacon."
"He said that? What did you do about it? It was your baby daughter he was talking to."
"He always said that to her, he wouldn't hurt her, only slap her, but she was always whingeing. He usually made her stop. She loved him."
"But Kim is thirteen months old and she had very serious injuries which the Consultant confirmed were inflicted that Friday night. What have you got to say about that?"
"I don't know. She was OK on the Sunday morning but she didn't wake us up as usual by throwing her toys at me; that was when I wondered if she was all right."
"She was far from all right, she had an arm fractured in four places. Did you look at her arms?"
"Yes, they were swollen and bruised."
"Did that worry you?"
"No, she always bruised easily. Debbie's children had fallen on her in the week."

"Is it true that you dragged Kim across the floor on Friday night?"
"No. I dragged her across the stairs."
"Why?"
"I panicked."
"What about?"
"She wouldn't listen to me."
"But she's only a baby, did you not understand that?"
"She has to learn. I was frustrated by her."
"Are you concerned about her now?"
"Yes."
"Why haven't you visited her in hospital?"
"I didn't have the money. I didn't know I could go. The social workers didn't tell me I could visit her. I thought she'd been taken for good."
"What do you want to happen now?"
"I want Kim back. I didn't mean to hurt her. I love her but she won't do as I tell her. I want the social workers to show me how to be a good mother."

The girl's mother stands up and shouts before anyone can stop her.
"You can't have her back, You're not fit to be a mother. I should have finished you off at birth, you've never been any good. You won't listen to me. You've never listened to me." She sobs.
The clerk tells her to sit down, the social worker goes to her, comforts her. The girl in the witness box starts to shout out.
"I never was good enough for you. You never gave me anything."
The chairman of the bench says "The court will adjourn for 30 minutes."
The three Magistrates stand, turn and walk away.
The clerk follows pressing the red button on her desk that lights up the sign on the door "Court in Progress."

# In the Village

1.
Nora tells me she has a fungicidal foot. Not a suicidal foot I'm glad to hear. It's all swollen up and when she saw the doctor he said it was through wearing vinyl shoes, there being no escape for the sweat. Nora said he told her to wear leather shoes or no shoes. As she tells me this I notice she's wearing a brown pair of vinyl shoes. "Why don't you wear leather shoes?" I ask. "Oh well," she says, "these look like leather don't they, with imitation grain, the doctor will never notice the difference." I tell her that her fungicidal foot won't get better in that case. She says, "It will because the shoes look just as good as leather ones."

2.
Just behind the factory set back in the field they say a German man lives on his own, he's been there since 1947. He was there before the factory and they say he's a Nazi war criminal; it was he who saw the end to thousands of lives. "Of course you can't prove it," the plumber said, "and there's not much anyone can do about it." They say he never goes out but when he does buy potatoes at the village shop they give him green ones.

3.
I ring up to order my Christmas meat.

"I'm just finishing the ironing," says the butcher's wife, "but I'll take down the order. George has broken his shoulder," she says. "Terrible—he can't move until the 23rd."

"He was in the abattoir, had gone down the steps. His feet went one way and his body went the other. He was unconscious on the floor for some hours even though the other man was down there too. He had the grinding machine on, couldn't hear him moan."

"When he got home he took the bandages off and started work again for the Christmas meat—he collapsed with pain. Now he's strapped up again but he's undone it twice. He can't believe that a butcher like him can be laid up at Christmas, trussed up like a turkey for three weeks with no guarantee of freedom."

I enquire about capons.

"Oh no, they have withdrawn them," she says, "they used to put pellets in their head to turn them off female birds, save their energy for the table, but now they've discovered the hormones react in a funny way."

"Tell George we hope he's soon better," I say.

"Thanks," she says, "he's under my feet all day, fussing with his arm in the air. I wish he could have a pellet, I can tell you."

## Luxury Goods

His father was a broad man, wide but tall as well. A large man. Solid. Ran his life by the book. A VAT inspector. His death was sudden, unexpected but not dramatic. He simply died while everyone else slept.

"When Bobby and I went to the Undertakers with Dad's measurements we saw to it that the coffin was a good oak. None of your Sapele or Teak." "Will it make it a luxury good?" Mother asked. "If it's classed as a luxury item we'll have to pay VAT on it; Dad told me that."

Bobby and I told her not to worry but the Undertaker told us that "dying is considered an essential item. It was classed," he told us confidentially, "along with women's sanitary attire." He shuffled uneasily, his face glowing, "although you can't get away without death or bleeding it is classified, nonetheless, as a luxury good."

We had a headstone and entered the name in the Book of Remembrance.

We paid VAT on both.

"What would Dad have said about it?" cried Mum. "He tried hard to avoid paying VAT himself. Always said that anything that was a luxury good was avoidable. VAT is strictly for the stupid, Barbara. He would have been so cross. Strictly for the stupid." "And for stiffs and bleeding women," Bobby added.

## Queuing

Queuing in front of me in the Sainsbury's checkout the slim dark-haired woman wears overalls. Nylon beige with gingham inset. She has a shopping trolley with chrome handles. The aisles are so cramped we can barely get our shopping through them.

"Good of Mr Sainsbury to give us so much room, given the money we spend in his shop," the woman in the queue shouts out. "The girl at the till shouts back, "Started at 6 a.m. finishing at. 6.00 p.m., haven't I? They're going to knock this store down and move into one of the big superstore spaces out of town. It suits me here you see, I can just about walk it. That's why I do my shopping in bits so I can carry it meself. I work for next to nothing for being on my feet all day."

Another cashier, young schoolgirl, acned face, label on her breast saying *Frankie* rings her bell, puts up her hand holding a packet of fish fingers. "85p," says the other girl. "I reckon I know everything in this store, I've been here a year. It's not been an easy year. I'm on my own you see. Two children at home, both waiting for me to get home now, they get worried if I'm not back. I'm their only security now. 14 and 10 they are. It's a lonely life. I have to run after work to get back to them, run with me shopping." The girl at the next isle rings her bell again raising a tin of pilchards above her head. "42p," shouts the other woman. "Sometimes I'm cashing these things in my sleep." Finally it's her turn and she piles up her groceries on the desk showing her staff pass as she pays. "Good luck love," says the younger woman. "I'm no need to worry about me. I'm quite content now he's gone, set up home with a manageress from Richards Shops didn't he, she's welcome to him and his snoring. Anyway she had a face like a cream cake." The girl starts on the next shoppers trolley, holds up a packet of biscuits as she rings the bell. "24p, love," says the woman as she leaves pushing her shopping trolley in front out. The price on the side says 56p. She winks and says, "Getting my own back on Mr Sainsbury, I am."

## Sharply Across the Top of the Head

The mother's case was simple. She wanted the child returned to her. In the evidence she claimed that life was now better. She had changed, now happily married to a man who didn't beat her; secure housing. What she didn't say was that she loved the child.

The Local Authority evidence said that adoption was in the best interests of the child seeing how the relationship between the mother and her child had always been poor. They claimed that even now the mother's life was in turmoil and that the man whom she had married had a record for injuring children and women.

In cross-examination the mother's barrister asked the social worker whether the child had been happy since coming into care. In truth the social worker said that the child had cried easily and constantly and suffered from a quick temper; she also shook with fear if she wet her knickers.

In cross-examination of the mother the Local Authority barrister inquired why the child should shake if she wet her knickers. The mother said she could not think why it would be so since if ever the child did wet her knickers she would simply tap her hand with a stick.

The barrister went on to say that witnesses could be called who would say that they had seen the mother holding the child out of the sixth-storey flat in which she lived by her ankles and that also scalds had been found on the soles of the child's feet. People who knew about it said the mother did it to teach the child a lesson. When asked about it the mother broke down.

In her evidence the mother said that her relationships were now stable and happy but later agreed that her new husband had recently left when she asked him to mend the Hoover. He had now returned. She agreed that he was a good man and that although he had accidentally injured children in the past he had now changed and would be a good father.

When asked if had ever injured her, she said that he had hit her but only once, sharply across the top of her head with a cricket bat because she had lied to him. The mother added, "I hadn't lied but I often look as though I am lying, I can't help that can I."

## That's How

We are standing by the baby-food counter looking at the tins and jars, the rusks and bibs. A mother, shopping has a pushchair with a sleeping tiny baby and a walking baby toddler who has grabbed armfuls of tins and is spreading them on the floor, a racing round older boy too who has taken one of the baby bikes from the display unit and is careering it between the Saturday shoppers' legs. The tiny baby stirs and starts to cry. "Oh Jesus," the mother says. "There's nine months between each of these; you want to try that." The walking baby has now taken off all the bibs from the shelves to add to her pile and is making for the plastic pants. They slide easily in a devastating pile before her. "How old is the baby?" I ask. "He's two months now, was two months prem. He's been such a worry I never thought he'd make it. He's had one thing after the other, chest infections, collapsed lungs. I had a Caesarean and couldn't move for two days. He was on special care and they wanted me to feed him, I couldn't. I didn't want to. I felt too tired out. I thought I'd recover first and then go and see him but the nurses wanted me to go straight away, I didn't feel ready for him for another two months. But there he was so I did my best, but I kept on crying every time I saw him. I didn't have one card sent to me. No one even knew I'd had a baby. My husband is a lorry driver, he's gone for four days when he does the Scottish trips. This time he was in Italy and had gone for ten days. My other two were with my neighbour. I was that low. Then, when I checked his pockets when he got home I found he had been staying in the red light district with a whore. He told me I was wrong but I'm not daft." The older boy rams his mother legs with the car. "Bloody hell, just finish me off why don't you," she screams.

# Without Blinking

Mrs C gives evidence. She is barely 20, she wears a blue nylon suit and high heels, very short hair, dark. She speaks easily and loudly.

"How long have you been married, Mrs C?"
"5 years."
"A happy 5 years?"
"On and off."
"What have the difficulties been about?"
"We had personal problems and rows, he wouldn't understand that it was difficult to keep the place tidy with four of us in one room."
"For some of the period after living in one room you were hospitalised and very ill. Did Mr C understand your problems with health?"
"Yes, he understood."
"How long were you having disagreements about the standard of housework?"
"About 4 years."
"So you were always arguing about it?"
"Yes."
"What personal problems did you have?"
"They are personal."
"Your sex life?"
"Yes. That and the housework and being in one room, the four of us, him, the child, me and his mother."

## Which We Weren't

"Talking about death," said the accountant, "which we weren't, I remember when I lived in Hythe as a child the old thick waxed gas capes. This old dear who lived on the front used to wear hers all the time; there was no need, they were terrible things. Hot and heavy and sticky. When her husband died she put him under the bed and told no one. But people knew; they suspected he'd gone. He'd never been very strong and when they didn't see him they wondered. Several people tried to get in the house but she'd never let them in, just came to the door in her cape shouting for them to go away and to leave her and her husband alone. She said she was all right, didn't need a doctor, that he'd never looked better in his life."

"People left it for a while, a few weeks actually, then she had to go out one day and when they saw she had gone they took the front door off its hinges and put their gas capes over their mouths and went in. Under the bed they found him dead as a dodo."

"A number of the men were sick. I was watching from the beach side of the road. When the old girl came back she ran into the house screaming from all the windows. "Someone's stolen my husband, Help, help."

I said that it must have been frightening for him as a child.

"No," he said, "I always found it quite amusing, quite amusing."

"These figures of yours don't add up here," said the accountant.

"Talking of humour," I said, "which we weren't."

## Achilles Heel

In the harbour there was a boat, a yacht more accurately, which had been named Grandson. She wondered, was this yacht instead of a grandson, or perhaps because of a grandson or for a grandson. It was maybe none of those and, in truth, she would never know and what did it matter, people had lives and ideas that no one knew about, for sure.

Truth was she felt that usually she knew too much about people's lives, the detail, the ups and mostly the downs. What he had said, what she had done and when the police had been called and when they left and what the children saw. Always it was about the children. Problem was that the children didn't get a look-in half the time, there was no room for thinking about how they might feel, stuck trying to make sense of it and where they stood in the muddle of it all. It wasn't about the children, it was about how the adults might use them to muster up support for their own cause.

She found herself saying the Bob Dylan words, "She just punched my eyelids and smoked my cigarette." Or was it the other way round, punching the cigarette and smoking the eyelids, she would find out.

But, here she was on holiday and already she had been thinking of what something meant. Grandson........., maybe one day she would have one of those herself. But for now she could stretch out, pause between the responsibility of her own children and supporting the next generation. Sitting on the lounger at the small beach in what was called "A Beach Club Resort" she read the newspaper and did some of the quick crossword. What could 8 Across be?—Orange cushion. Plato's life, an egg joke perhaps... Such clues required an education far different to her own.

A Brazilian family, a few yards away sat or rather splayed across the seats, their enormous frames bulging from the loungers and seats. They were eating chips and the adults were smoking. After a few minutes they ordered more chips from the passing waiter. The smaller of the two boys in the family cried out as his mother wrenched an electronic game from his hands and he started to wail. The mother was firm and held on to the gadget, the father remained motionless, smoking. Across and to her right, two men laughed and combed one another's hair, a young couple lay sleeping rolled up in each other's arms. She noted the man was however eyeing a young woman's bottom at the next table as she walked by in her thong. The resting woman was strong in her lover's arms, innocent that his thoughts were far from being upon her.

An hour later she walked down the main street and sat at the Demetrious Fountain Café. No fountain, also no Demetrious but a café of a kind, and as she approached a seat in the sunshine a large man with even taller companion approached. The taller man had his arm resting along his companion's shoulder. After a formal greeting the pair sat down and she watched them. She was almost instantly aware that the larger man was disabled and his friend was caring for him. The pair ordered drinks and food before her and she watched as the smaller, older man took charge. He was, she now noted, much older and that his companion was perhaps his son or younger brother. Over the next hour she struck up a conversation with the older man; he told her that he lived locally and that his brother was visiting him, this time for five months, usually he came for three, this time longer to give his mother some respite. She was old and tiring, herself. His brother, he explained, had been injured in his brain at a young age in a bike accident and was very damaged. He could function well mentally but needed constant guidance, especially in walking and talking, but his arm was dead and unless he could rest it he could not walk. He was fine, but the guidance was key, he explained. She noted that during the meal the younger man barely spoke but laughed and appeared happy and was prepared to be helped. As the pair left the café she saw that the taller man leant very heavily upon his brother, that his arm, his huge arm, his very dead arm, weighing maybe 5 stone or more leant upon his brother and that together they walked home from the café like yoked oxen, steady, slow, very slow, the older man clearly burdened. The younger, knowing this, walking slowly.

# Easter Holiday London Trip

On the Circle Line in the Easter holidays a young family boards the train at Oxford Circus. The children are aged about 2½ and 5. The little boy sits next to me with his father at his other side. He is sitting on his knees and his hand is between his legs. His sister and mother sit opposite. I want to go to the toilet, I want to do a wee wee, the little boy says. You definitely want to go now son? his daddy asks, why didn't you tell me before we got on the train? We will have to get off now. No, I don't want to go now, the boy says. His sister pipes up, why does he always cause so much trouble when we go out? He's not, the mother says. Yes, he is, he is, she add, anyway I want something to eat. A few minutes pass and we are now at Euston Square. I've got to do a wee wee now, now, the little boy says. We have to get off and go the father says. The boy shakes his head fiercely and repeats that he no longer wants to go.

The mother has given her daughter the remains of a McDonald's which she starts to eat hungrily. A few seconds later her mouth puffs up while she makes vomiting sounds. Are you going to be sick? asks her mother. No, she says, I'm fine. The little boy is now clutching his genitals again and is jumping up and down. The father is holding a drink carton and says, We are all going to have to get off and you are going to have to go in this cup. I won't go in the cup, the boy says, I don't want to go any more, I will be all right, I will be all right. The mother says, We will be getting off soon. The girl has started to choke; the mother offers her the drink. I don't want that, she says, he might go to the toilet in it. But he hasn't, the mother says. The child continues to make gagging sounds and the little boy jumps up and down.

I get off.

## What She Said

What she said, when I asked why she hadn't seen the children, was that she had meant to but hadn't, she had wanted to but then as it had been so long that she thought it best to stay away. Then she cried a bit and I asked her if she wanted a tissue. "I want my f.....g kids," she said. I told her she needed to show the court that she was responsible now and could care for them properly. She looked out of the window. "Why don't you take someone else's kids away." Then she spat. As she walked away she turned back and shouted, "Anyway, you can have them, see if I care." I watched her angry back walk into the heavy doors.

When she came back she said that it wasn't me she was angry with. She told me that she had been twelve years old when her mum left her; she had never seen her since and hadn't wanted to see her anyway. "I can't be it, I can't love them enough."

She walks away pressing digits on her mobile phone as she walks out of the building. I watch her as she passes the hoardings on the roadside advertising milk.

## In Her Caravan

She has his photograph; it is a blurred picture of a tiny baby propped up by the Tampax box. She tells me she has no regrets. He had to go, what with her health and all that.
    Signs readily the paper to make him someone else's to love and restore back into focus.


## My Dad

will show you all up, taking the mickey out of him isn't a good
                          idea if you want to live a long time lady
he says as his pierced face
red and swollen leans into mine.
The gold ring is bent and he catches my eye
"costs you to look, want to kiss my arse?"
Walking away down the path
the dog on the leash barks, gets too close for comfort,
it's eating a Happy Meal.

## Danny

won't speak to me, runs round the room and then shakes the dolls by the throat, stares at me for a while and then writes on his left hand with biro "left." Throws sand for a while and then says he wants to sleep, drawing up the cover over his head, he then shouts out, "She left me."

## Susan

tells me she that this baby will be her fourth and that it is a boy again, that his father treats her like she was a film star. "Then he tells me I'm an old slag," she laughs.

"I got an infection in my privacy from him," Susan says and starts to cry. While she fumbles in her pocket for a tissue her phone falls to the floor. "I was on the phone to the doctor about this pain but he hung up on me."

Susan wipes her face on her sleeve. "When I went to hospital no one visited me, not that I wanted anyone to hold my hand, but you never know, do you, it might be OK if they did."

## When He Asked Her

She had been standing by the photocopying machine when he'd asked her. Would you come to Greece with me, Jay, I've got two tickets and it's a three-star hotel from the 3$^{rd}$ August for two weeks. I'd like it for you to come. She didn't hesitate; *will I need malaria tablets?* He was confused by this response and said he'd find out and that they'd maybe talk about it on Friday when he picked her up. She had known Connor for four months, liked him, he worked in IT Support, they had met in the canteen. He had seen for her several days, wondering if he could speak to her. She was always surrounded by other people. On this particular day, Thursday 17 March, her friend Becky had gone to collect knives and forks and she had been left on her own. He seemed very tall then, she had noticed that. She also noticed that his shoes seemed far too big for his feet, *like boats* her gran would say, they did literally float away from the sides of his feet. He'd come up to her at the table just as Becky came back. Hi Jay, he had said, how is it in Finance? It's fine, she said, a bit boring, but I'm getting there, the girls have been very helpful; not sure they all like me though. Connor asked if she needed any extra help. He then said, *If you feel like you need it, do you want to meet for a drink on Friday? I'll be at the Fox at 7.00 p.m.* She said that she would. Becky had laughed out loud and pointed at Connor's shoes as he walked away. *Shh* said Jay, *I like him.* Since then they had seen each other twice a week, sometimes three times, she'd been to his home, he'd been to hers. He had a Renault Clio which his father had given to him when he was 18. *I'm lucky really* he said, *spoilt rotten, that's me.* That was all he'd said about his family. He'd met her mum, *Pleased to meet you Mrs B,* he'd said and held out his hand. He looked her straight in the eye as if he had nothing to hide and she liked that about him.

    She was 20 when he asked her to go to Zante with him. She told her mum. *Who's paying? It will be expensive, you mark my words.* It's Connor's treat, she said. *There is no such thing as treats* her mother had said. *Everyone wants something in return.* Her grandma was the worst. *Don't go running off with any Arabs.*

*Bring us back 400 Bensons and don't drink anything but bottled water, don't even clean your teeth in it, don't eat no fruit nor salad, if you vomit a lot dunk your head in the sea. Don't let those Muslims get you to eat their meat, wear ones of those hats or blow you up either.* Her mother had then added as she turned away, *don't give anyone your credit card, not even in a bank, ring me every day and don't get pregnant.* With her mother's words ringing in her ears she wondered if she had known that she had already slept with Connor. It had not been good; she had regretted it and he knew it, she always did somehow.

He picked her up at 4.10 a.m. outside her house; his friend Martin drove them in his truck, it was on his way round the M25. She clambered into the front seat. It was very dark and very cold and her bare feet in the thonged sandals seemed out of place and she wished now she was wearing her Ugg boots instead. Connor was wearing his football shirt, jeans and for reasons she could not understand, new even huger boots which made his feet seem larger than ever. He was excited and he cuddled her against him as the truck drew away and into the darkness. Got your passport and everything then Jay? Connor asked. Got your bikini and your pill said Martin as he nudged Connor and slapped his thigh. Martin had originally been planning to go to Zante with Connor but he had backed off at the last minute.

At the airport hoards of people were queuing at the desk. Connor held the tickets in one hand with his case and he held her hand with the other, he was sweating and seemed anxious. Jay asked him how many times he had been abroad. Once with me parents, once with the school and now with you. That'll be the best trip of them all he said and she kissed him. In the departure lounge Jay looked at his new boots, They had writing down one side and were yellow with huge laces coming out of metal rings. When did you get those boots Connor? She laughed as she spoke and he looked upset Don't you like them then? I think you might get a bit hot that's all she said and maybe not so good in the sand.

On the plane Connor had a beer. *It's only 9 o'clock* she said. *I'm on holiday now Jamie and it's all to play for, it's all to play for,* he had said. Jay read her magazine while Connor listened to his iPhone. He moved his feet up and down with the music and sometimes whistled quite loudly. *Can you keep still for a bit? Also your boots are so hard on the floor it's making the woman in front turn round* she said but Connor closed his eyes and went to sleep.

Once through passport control they waited for their baggage. They seemed to wait for a very long time; other passengers from the flight had their bags; Connor had his, but hers had not arrived. They waited by an area that someone told them was Help Desk, it was signed in odd hieroglyphics. The man was unhelpful and said *No problem* repeatedly. It was impossible to tell him that it was a problem but they gave him their names and the tour-company details. Connor was blasé, you can wear my clothes babe, you look hot in anything. Jay was upset that the holiday had started like this and she began to recall things in her suitcase that she might never see again. She was relieved that her pill was in her handbag; it was wasn't it?

The tour rep swept them up. You've kept everyone waiting now let's get you on the coach. All eyes were on them as they stumbled up the steps of the huge bus that was filled to capacity. They had to sit apart and Jay was sat next to a young boy carrying a large boomerang, Connor was at the back of the coach sitting with a group of girls; she could hear them all laughing. The boy with the boomerang was looking out of the window, she studied his thin legs in his shorts and his enormous boomerang clutched tightly on his lap. The boy's mother spoke to her, *Where you going pet, which hotel you at?* Jay told her that she didn't know as her boyfriend had arranged it all. *We're at the Beach Shack again* the woman said, *lovely there you can watch all the men's bums as they go by with their beers, that's what I'm looking forward to, pet.*

The coach had been going for some time and it seemed to be getting dark. Finally it lurched to a stop by a hotel, *The Miramar* shouted the rep. Several groups got off and there was now room on the coach to sit with Connor. She wished the family a happy holiday and moved to a window seat but Connor did not catch her eye he was still chatting to the girls.

The tour rep came on the coach and announced there would be a short delay of ten minutes while the driver changed over. Across the coach aisle a young woman with very short dark hair turned and smiled at Jay and started to speak. Within minutes she had told important parts of her life story. Jay found people often told her things, sometimes things she would rather not have known. This girl spoke almost non-stop. *There are two factories 10 minutes from where I live, that's Waterlooville near Portsmouth. My name is Kiki and I live with my mum and stepdad. I've only been back there for six months. Before that I was living with my boyfriend until he cheated on me for the third time.* Jay nodded and said she was sorry. Kiki went on, *Mum was okay about me returning, she said it would be company given that Chris my stepfather was usually out. I had always got on well with him, he lived with us since I was three. Chris worked in Portsmouth's Sainsbury's in charge of stockkeeping or something, he moved things around on forklift trucks. He had not been married he said that before he met and married my mum he had no children. Chris liked photography. He had fallen out, or so he said, with his own family but we never knew why. He just sort of laughed over it whenever the subject came up and then went quiet. Mum worshipped Chris, he was so different from my real dad who was never interested in mum or in me for that matter and spent his time either asleep or watching football. He was in the pub a lot too, it was hard to know how my mum and he got together at all but they did. Mum used to say it was because his dad had an allotment and that she always trusted gardeners. My dad had never touched a blade of grass let alone a spade so I never would work that out. Grandad died before I was born but everyone said he was a gentleman.* Jay turned round to see if she could catch Connor's eye but he seemed to be asleep on the shoulder of one of the girls who was laughing with her friends. Kiki noticed this and asked, *Is that your boyfriend, looks like he won't be for much longer then?* Jay was feeling slightly sick, she turned back and looked out of the window into the Mediterranean darkness, a man was rolling a barrel of beer along the ground.

Kiki went on, *the other day Chris told mum and I that something really bad had happened to him when he was a kid and it was the first time he had spoken about it. He said that it was so bad that if we knew about it we probably wouldn't love him any more. Mum told him that nothing could be that bad and he said that it was, but he then wouldn't say any more. The factory where I work makes tin things, I'm on the assembly line and my friend Roz is five yards from me so we can chat and indeed chat we do. Roz is the sort of girl that everybody speak too, she has got a round face, a big smile and a birthmark across one ear which you can't see because her hair hides it but Roz is convinced that everyone can see it. She's got a little boy, Joe-Joe and she's a good mum. Her mum looks after Joe-Joe while she's at work. Joe-Joe doesn't have a dad. The only thing Roz will say about him is,* if I hadn't known him I wouldn't have had Joe-Joe, he was a bent bastard and that's all I want to say about it Kiki so don't ask no more OK love, OK? *I was keen to go on holiday but I didn't have anyone to go with me. I looked up lots of deals and when this one came up I told mum that I would pay for her if she came with me and she said I can't leave Chris, Kiki you know I can't. I asked her why she couldn't, she said, I just can't, that's all. It upset me a bit because the last time mum and I had been on holiday was well, basically well, never. Not just the two of us, not with dad, not with Chris and I would have liked that. I've seen families on holiday and they look confident and attractive, I suppose that we wouldn't look like that anyway.*

Jay wanted Kiki to stop, the girl never paused for breath. *I do think people will talk to me when I am away, it won't be that awkward when I'm on my own. Some people might ask and some people will just look at me and they might think that I'm a jilted honeymooner, it doesn't bother me, they can think all they like. I am not taking many clothes, you don't need them do you, not if it's hot. The thing I will take though is all my shoes but then they are quite heavy aren't they? I will take a book, not that I do a lot of reading, but it might make me feel less awkward in the restaurant having a book even if I don't open it, it gives you something to focus on. I always think that all the people I met on the plane going out are they on the plane coming back but I suppose you don't always meet the same people do you. I suppose the waiters might hit on me, but then they didn't before when I went to Frankie and Benny's with Roz on her birthday last year. They looked right through me like they could see my knickers. I'm staying on a resort. It looks nice, there's a pool and a bar called Sundowners. I shan't sunbathe that much because I could get cancer, I think it runs in our family. Do you think I talk too much by the way, some people say I do but it's all in me head and sometimes it needs turning out, do you know what I mean?*

Finally a driver stumbled into the seat and they were off again. He looked remarkably like the first driver but Jay was glad to be going again; she craned her neck round to see Connor coming down towards her. Again she heard them laughing and shouting out from the girls *See you later then.* Connor was flushed and happy as he fell into the seat next to Jay, *Those girls have got some brandy back there* he said. *Nice for you then, need not have come away just for me* Jay said. *Don't be daft* he said and kissed her; he smelt terrible. *Anyway,* he added, *they're at our hotel, The Acropolis, so we'll be seeing them.*

Five minutes later they were headed towards Reception; she felt ill thinking about her lost suitcase and wondering what she was going to do. The rep was no help at all. *Don't worry* she had said, *it happens all the time and if they don't bring it in three days you can get a voucher and buy some new clothes, not that you need many here it's so hot.*

Up in the room Connor spread out on the bed, his huge boots still on his feet, marking the white cotton sheet with mud. *Do take your boots off Con,* she asked. *That's not all I'm taking off,* he said, and grabbed hold of her. With his boots still on he was snoring within minutes while she lay smothered by him. Jay disentangled herself from Connor's bad breath and walked to the small balcony, watching the brilliant red sun go down across the bay. The view from the room was amazing. She was beginning to feel better about it all and the room was quite nice, spacious. Jay wanted to let her mum know she had arrived, she wouldn't let on about the suitcase yet, no point. It was then that she looked through her hand bag for her pills. Phew, they were there, but just three days' worth; she had put the other packet in the case, knowing she would take them to delay her period until she was home.

Connor finally was roused from his coma and they explored the hotel with its beautiful trees and scented flowers. It was close to the beach and they wandered about hand in hand. *Did you bring flip-flops Connor,* Jay asked him, *those boots are going to get hot.* Connor grabbed her and kissed her—*I will definitely be getting hot all right,* he said and laughed.

At the Beach Shack Reception Vivien asked the clerk if they were in the same shack as before, *Shack 17* she said, *we've had it every year.* Rob turned to her, *not that I would know about that. You were here last year Rob* she said *and you would have been here the year before but what happened?* Rob shrugged his shoulders and slumped down in an armchair. Liam stood next to his mum, he had hold of his little Trunkie and the boomerang. You go and sit with Rob, she said but Liam did not move. Finally the desk clerk said, *Madam you are not in 17 we have a roof repair there but we have 23. Is it the same as 17?* Vivien asked. *It's a tiny bit smaller* the clerk said, *but you will love it. What do you mean by smaller. Madam, it is just the one room like 17 but smaller, just one bedroom*, the clerk said, *plus the bathroom and the kitchen of course, there is one double bed and one single, come, I show you.* He took them out and he started to make his way. *That's not what we asked for*, Vivien was put out, *we wanted 17, we've always been in there, I've always been there, Liam loves it, he needs his own bedroom. We don't have, madam,* he said, *we don't have, hotel very full.* Rob stood up. *What's going on, you mean to say you haven't got what we have asked for, what I paid for, you haven't got it, chummy, have you?* Vivien did not say that she had paid for the holiday. *I think we have to go and look at it,* she said. *I for one am not sharing a room with anyone, they will have to do something different* shouted Rob as they walked off into the night following the man with the keys.

They made their way up past the other shacks which faced the beach, No. 17, it was true, was boarded up, the tarpaulin on the roof, the roof felt just flapping in the wind. No. 23 was not on the beach, it was a row back, but there was still a glimpse of the golden sand and the sea.

The clerk flew the door open in a sweeping elaborate gesture, *see it, lovely madam, it perfect, you will love and complimentary dinner is on Demitris, it no problem for you. I don't want complimentary dinner* said Rob *I want to stay in a place that we have paid for, that I have paid for, that has two rooms, one for us and one for him.* He gestured with his thumb towards Liam who was standing by the door. *I hope tomorrow we will be able to mend 17, be no problem*, said the clerk, *but tonight sir I invite you dinner on us and stay here*. Vivien was weary, *thank you very much we will do that*. *Well I'm not happy, not happy at all* Rob said and he walked out of the door. Vivien exchanged glances with Liam who looked away. *Go and put your things out on the bed, she said to Liam, sort out your pyjamas, find your swimming things for tomorrow, I'll be back in a minute, I'll find Rob*. Liam opened his trunkie and sat down on the bed and put his boomerang on the pillow. He noticed there were no blankets, just a thin sheet. He was pleased to be in the same room as his mum; that way he would be able to wake up and see her. He remembered the pool and the waves in the sea and the big breakfasts where he could help himself to milk through an urn-type thing. He wondered what they would be having for dinner and the thought of it then made him feel funny. He wasn't sure that he wanted dinner and he knew that Rob wouldn't let him take boomerang to the table. He kissed boomerang an extra three times. Outside he could hear his mother speaking to Rob.

Rob came into the room, glanced at Liam and went into the bathroom. A few seconds later he said, *I'm off to the bar. Wait for a minute, we'll all go with you,* mum said.. He turned and walked away. *I've put boomy into bed*, said Liam, *he's all tucked up*. Liam saw that his mother was crying.

# Neighbours

1.
First one neighbour is running, shouting, then she is screaming. I can't understand what she is saying or doing. Another neighbour rushes past her carrying a shotgun. There is much noise and five shots are fired. Following much movement towards the back of my neighbour's garden, other people from the forest have come too; they also are running. It is midday and normally there is not a soul about. They all stand around looking to the ground. I throw my hands into the air and say hello several times in Turkish, I then shout out *Pleased to meet you,* it being one of the few phrases I know other than *Mr Brown is an architect from Antalya.*

I am told that, unusually, two snakes were found slithering through the grass, dangerous snakes that could kill a person. My neighbour tells me to buy some special chemical powder to put all around the edges of my garden. The next day he hands me sack of it; it is bright yellow and I spend the day piling it on as instructed, a quarter of an inch thick. It it is hard to understand how anything would deter a snake, perhaps one is already living in my garden or indeed his long friends are planning to join him. I comply; nonetheless my usual open door to the garden is now closed at night.

2.
My friend in London tells me that her new neighbour has said some very strange things to her. He told her first of all, *I am glad you are like me with a total dislike of any degree of physical contact with another human being.* My friend was taken aback and responded by saying, oh actually I don't have that problem. He then said, *let me put it this way if you see two men kissing it looks horrific, if you see two women kissing it's truly ghastly, if you see a man and a woman kissing it's stomach-churning, I tend to look away.* He then added, *but then I worry what else I am going to see when I look away, I can't stand it, I'm relieved that you feel the same way.* He then went in and closed his door.

3.
My neighbour's daughter is 7 years old, I like to talk to her about the games she is playing. She usually plays on her own and I watch her talking to herself, bouncing a ball against the wall and running from one end of her garden to the other. I also see her sometimes climbing onto the roof of her father's shed. *What are you doing*, I ask her; she says, *I am pretending to be a chicken.* I ask her why; she says, *because I could then get eaten by my mummy and be back in her tummy.*

4.
A boy is brought to see me. His father says I have to fix him or he will have to go and live somewhere else as he is making his stepmother ill by his constant demands for attention and angry outbursts.

The boy plays in the sand, tells me how much he misses his brother who died two years ago. I ask him, *What would you wish for if you had a magic wand?* He says, *For people to smile and not to frown when they see me. The lady next door gave me a peach stone to plant in my garden, she said that by the time it had grown into a tree I would forget a lot of things that happened when I was little, do you think I will,* he asks?

5.
Frank tells me that when his dog dies he will die too. *How do you know this*, I ask. *Stands to reason doesn't it,* he says, *he'll need me to look after him in heaven.* I comment that Frank has been a farmer for over 60 years and has slaughtered animals and seen the births and deaths of thousands of lambs on Romney Marsh. *A dog is different,* he says, *part of me, my right hand and anyway I promised him.*

## Notes Towards Loss

1.
I don't mind about it but he does. Ben needs to go to sleep first or else he makes a noise that gets to mum so I go outside with him and put him in the buggy.

Sometimes he screams until he is blue and once he scratched my face but he didn't understand that I had to do it. I had to strap him in. There was a day last week when I hit him a bit, hit him hard because he has to learn things.

Mum hadn't taken her tablets yet so I made some tea for her and get her to lay down. When mum gets ill I help out more but then she doesn't notice things as she sleeps a lot. When she hears voices I take the radio to Pam's house next door as once she smashed it up. I put the cushions over the telly and the cloth over it as well.

Our dad's a bastard. Mum said that and that he didn't deserve to have a lad like me. He comes sometimes, says it's not right and then goes away. He did change Ben's nappy and rang the Social. We don't want them poking in here as one time the doctor made her go away and Ben was taken off me. No one knows how to get him off to sleep like me.

2.
When Steven said I smelt funny and that he wouldn't be my partner in PE I cried a bit and then I ran off into the trees. It was dark there they didn't find me

Miss Bartlett took me in the toilets and washed my face and gave me some shorts. She slipped a banana in the pocket at break but I don't like them much.

Our mum went mad when that woman came to our house and said we should have sheets on our bed again. She made mum clean up and she brought things with her.

It was better when we had the light-bulb in our room but Brian smashed it with his shoe from the top bunk when he got sent upstairs. He weed in the corner of our room again and now it's brown on the floor and rotting a bit.

3.
I like to chat and I know that I shouldn't do it. I'm always following people around I don't like being on my own I know I get in the way and I do want to be good. I am good, but I chat too much, I know that. Leave it out, my mum says, for Christ's sake leave it out for a minute.

I don't know what I get wrong but then I do. Maybe I am bad that's it, I am not good at things so I don't sleep much, mostly I play in my room.

When Uncle George lived here I'd sit on his lap a lot, no one said it was wrong, he said it was good.

But I don't like being on my own and when I don't sleep I listen on the stairs. I heard them say that Uncle George was locked up.

# Stories from the Contact Centre

## One

It was the second Saturday in the month and Philip went to get Danny out of bed early. "Come on, Danny, we've got to get to the shops to see if we can get you those new school shoes and then we're going on to meet mum." Danny reached out for his Gameboy and started playing on it as he tucked down further into the covers. Philip asked him again, "Come on Danny, you've got to get up now, and when I say now I mean now." Danny turned over to face the wall while still playing with his Gameboy. Philip pulled the covers off the bed and found that the bed was wet. "Danny, how many times have I told you, tell me if you've wet the bed." "But I haven't," said Danny. "You have son, you're laying in it, it's all wet, get yourself in the bathroom and I'll strip the bed again, get in the shower and make sure you wash." Danny went off into the bathroom still playing on the Gameboy. Philip stripped the beds and on the way out he stuck a downward sad face on Danny's star chart.

At the shops Danny was helpful, choosing his new shoes without difficulty. After lunch Philip reminded him they were going to see Mum. "I wish you could stay there, Dad, I wish you could just be there when I see Mum." "But you know that I can't," said Philip. "She comes to see you, not me."

As soon as they arrived at the Contact Centre Philip looked around and saw that Sarah was not there. "She won't be long, let's just wait a little bit." After about five minutes she arrived. Philip saw that she looked tired than ever. She was carrying two big bags. Philip hoped that she was not going to give Danny any more clothes or toys but had brought something for them to play with today. Danny's eyes lit up when he saw his Mum and he went over to her and she cuddled him. She then started shouting at Philip before he could leave, "Why do you dress him in these clothes, why do you dress him like there is something wrong with him, why do you not dress him in the clothes I bring, eh eh, answer me that?" Philip said, "Let's not have a row about this now Sarah, he's just wearing his ordinary clothes, these are the clothes he likes to wear." Danny put his hands up to his ears, he really didn't want this. Philip said, "I'll be just waiting upstairs, okay."

Sarah liked to do jigsaws and over the next two hours they did nothing but a big complicated jigsaw together in the middle of the room. Everyone seemed to look at them. Now and again Sarah would shout out to one of the contact supervisors, "You tell me why my son is so thick." He hated it when she behaved like this and the supervisors spoke to her quietly, calming her down. She always apologised to Danny as she cuddled him, "You know I don't mean it, I just get frustrated." At the end of contact he was relieved but always sad to see her go. He noticed that the scars on her eye from the operations were beginning to heal. It was embarrassing, Danny knew that his mother looked odd, and feeling guilty and remembering made him feel sick. Since she set fire to her hair it had taken him a long time to get used to how she looked nowadays. He hugged her and sometimes he wished that they could stay together like that just the two of them forever, but then he knew that it would be too hard.

### Two

The journey down from Preston had taken five hours. Bill had picked them up in the van at 6.30 a.m. He said, "It'll save your legs waiting at the bus stop, they're only every hour and if they've a mind they don't come at all." They were grateful. Jean had packed a flask of coffee, some sandwiches and a piece of cake. She knew how Alfie felt faint very quickly if he didn't eat regularly. He wouldn't manage that, not with the travelling as well. The upset of it was bad enough, to think that they had to book up to see their own grandchildren in a place where other people had to watch them, it wasn't right. They'd never done anything wrong, they loved the kids, they'd never harm them. A bitch of a daughter-in-law had made their lives hell. Jean had known from the moment she saw her that she was trouble, "all front, that's what she is, all front." She remembered Alfie saying, "You can say that again and quite a front it is too on her, if I may say so." Jean had thrown him a look. "You wait and see if I'm not right," she said, "that girl means nothing but harm to our Richard, I can tell it."

When the girls were born Jean had been thrilled with her two little granddaughters who lived three streets away and Marcia would bring the girls over after school at least three times a week. She had a part time job in the video shop. "It gets me out mum," she'd say. Richard had a job at the building suppliers and Jean thought they were just an ordinary family like everyone else. Then one Friday afternoon Richard came home. It was unusual; he never had a day off work. "What's the matter?" Jean asked him. "Nothing, can you have the girls for the weekend, I'm taking Marcia away." "Well that's new," said Jean, "but yes, I will." When the girls came that weekend they weren't their usual happy little selves. "Mummy and Daddy have been arguing," said Katie. "Shouting all night, Daddy says Mummy's got a boyfriend." Susie added, "I heard her kissing someone on the phone, she kissed her mobile phone." At the end of the weekend Jean watched as their car drew up outside and Richard got out to collect the girls. "Where's Marcia?" "Mum I need to tell you something," said Richard. "I can't find Marcia, I've been down South this weekend to look for her, she's left me, she's met a bloke from London and she says she's not coming back, what's worse is that she's coming tomorrow to take the girls."

Weeks and months went by and Richard came round for his evening meal now that he was on his own. He heard things, how she was accusing him of being drunk all the time and never helping with the children, him seeing other women, how the girls didn't want to see him. That was two years ago and it had all gone from bad to worse. Things happened that Jean had never even dreamed of knowing about. Katie had said her granddad Alfie had touched her while she was having a bath and that Katie said she never wanted to see granddad again. The police had come and taken Alfie away, it was terrible, it made his diabetes go haywire. Jean thought that the world couldn't get worse, he loved those little girls. She knew that Alfie would never have touched Katie, he was just not that sort of man, but then some days she'd wonder and she'd think back on things she had put away, it made her think twice but she never said. And now they had to go down to see the girls in a contact centre in a place where other people could watch what they did, what they said. It had taken two court hearings and them being interviewed to get this far. They would have to make the best of it.

Jean had never been to London; Alfie had, in the lorry, but Jean hadn't thought much of it as they went on the Underground to get through to the other side of London before finding their way down South to the place where the girls were now living with their mum and her fancy new man called Todd. From what Jean heard, Todd took the biscuit. He had a brand new BMW car and he worked as a manager for a cinema complex. They got to the door of the contact centre, Alfie said that he felt a bit funny. Jean had given him his sandwiches and the coffee on the train, "Have a seat," she said, "you'll feel better in a minute, it's all the upset." Once inside he did seem to perk up a bit. The woman in charge made them a cup of tea and told them to wait upstairs where there was a comfortable settee. When the girls came in Jean thought that her heart would break, their stick-like arms and legs were just as they'd always been; they were wearing thin dresses, it was November. The girls were all over her, she never wanted to let them go. They spoke to Alfie but she noticed that neither of them went near him, that wasn't how things used to be. Jean asked if they'd seen their Dad. "We see him every day," said Katie, "of course we see him." It was then that Jean realised they were now calling Todd Dad. "I meant your real Dad," said Jean. "Oh him," said Katie, "no, we don't see him any more, mum says he don't send her no money." At the end of their time with the girls Jean thought again that her heart would break, she watched them walk out the door without turning back to wave, like they always had done in the past.

# Three

When Julie told him she was pregnant he was without doubt the happiest man in the world. When she told him two days later that it was twins he went straight to the pub and got plastered. When he came back Julie didn't look too pleased. He explained in a way, as he always did with a sideways lopsided grin. "It's not every day a man gets to be told he's going to be the dad of twins." After the boys were born things changed. Julie got tired and he spent more time at any pub. Things weren't great between them; they went to a counsellor and he promised to stop drinking. Instead he had cans at home. "I'll just have one more while the footie's on," he'd say to Julie. He loved the boys, Robbie and Billy, he'd take them out as proud as anything in the double buggy while Julie could have a clear up at home. Only once did he take them in the pub; somehow Julie found out. "Do that again, I'll leave you." He worshipped Julie, she'd been the best thing that had ever happened to him and he wasn't about to blow it.

Three years later when Julie started working he looked after the boys more and more, he'd pick them up two nights after nursery school and bring them home, give them their tea and wait for Julie. Just once in a while he'd buy a can or two at the offie. "You've been drinking," she said when she got home. "No I haven't, you're imagining it," he would say. One day Julie came home and said she'd had enough; either she would go or he should go but it would be easier if he went because she would have to look after the boys. He pleaded his case and said he would go to Alcoholics Anonymous, he would stop drinking. Julie said, "It's ten times too often; just go, and take your bottle opener with you." He knew she meant it.

After Julie left everything slid. He lost his job, but he did see the boys. Julie would bring them round regular as clockwork and he loved his time with them but once, or was it twice, he couldn't remember now, he'd had a can or two during the time he'd had with them. Billy had told his mum. The next thing he knew they were all in court and Julie was saying that he was an unfit parent to see them on his own. Now he had to see the boys at the contact centre. They always came, never let him down, not like some of the children and some of the stories he heard with the other dads. Julie always made sure the boys came and they always looked spick and span. "How's your mum?" he'd ask the boys. They would tell him, sometimes he didn't want to hear their answer, sometimes he couldn't look when he saw her in the doorway, she looked so beautiful. Once she came over to speak to him, the boys liked that. He touched her arm, it was soft and warm. "You look good," he said. When Julie looked at him she saw that his front teeth were missing. She couldn't repay the compliment. When the boys left the centre with their mum he went into the pub across the road. "A quick half to see me on my way," he would say to the barman, who now knew him as a regular.

## Four

The day she found out that Mike was leaving her Barbara told the children, "Your dad's found another family to live with, he doesn't love us any more." Emily, who was 14, told her mum, "I never want to see him again." Robert, who was 10, worshipped his daddy, sat and cried. "I never meant to hurt you, Barbara," said Mike, "I never meant to hurt you, I just never felt like you needed me." Barbara had needed Mike, she'd needed him very much, it's just that she wasn't a person who could show her feelings very easily. It had always been her problem, even the girls at work had said to her, "Loosen up a bit, Barb, liven up, get yourself going." She was just not like that. When she met Mike she thought her world had just started. He saw in her the things that she wanted people to know about her without needing to tell them, and now he had left her, just like her dad had. It was all happening again.

It was two years Mike had been gone now and Emily still refused to see her dad. Robert had been seeing a psychologist, he wasn't doing well at school, he got into trouble. They'd all been to see a therapist, Mike as well. Emily had spat at him in the family therapy session, she was angry. "You've got your nice little family with Carol and your new baby and Carol's children, Rachel and Sally, it's all cosy wosy, you don't need us anymore," she had said. Her father had said nothing, Barbara was, as usual, speechless. Towards the end of the session Emily had turned on her mum and had said, "You should say something, you should stop being so dumb." Those words had hurt her, she knew that Emily was right but she couldn't do anything about it. Now Emily had agreed to see her dad at a contact centre and she and Robert went off to see him. When they'd gone Barbara went up and looked in Emily's bedroom; she was sure she was seeing a boy. She was sure she was sleeping with him.

At the contact centre Mike broke down when he saw his children. He was so happy, "Don't you bloody start, we have enough with Mum," said Emily. Robert just held his dad's hand. "I didn't leave you," said Mike, "it isn't you I left, just remember that." But Emily wasn't listening, she was looking at her mobile phone; there was a text there for her. She would be seeing him later and so what that he was a married man with a kid.

## Five

The day mum took them all to the refuge was when a bit of the world ended. He saw it on the news, an aeroplane had gone into a big tower in the middle of America. Everyone was crying, everything had come to an end. It was all there was on the TV, even at the refuge, the lady was talking about how awful it was and what a tragedy and how many people had been killed. He wasn't sure how people had come to be killed but he knew that his dad had done it. He'd seen Dad hitting Mum more times than he could remember, now he slept next to his mum and he could always look after her. Sometimes he heard his mum crying in her sleep. She wasn't awake but she was crying while her eyes were closed and he would shake her to wake her up but she didn't. He didn't know why his mum had to take pills to help her sleep, she seemed to do that fine on her own.

It was a long time before he had his own bedroom in their own house. When he did he didn't like it. He wished he was back next to his mum again. It was a shame because she'd had it decorated out in Liverpool stripes with a Liverpool bedspread. He remembered that his dad supported Arsenal. He knew that his mum had to go to Court a lot and a lady had come to talk to him. She asked him about seeing his dad. He didn't want to see him, not after he'd killed all those people, not after he'd hurt his mum, not after he'd made a piece of the world come to an end. Lots of times people came and told him that he had to go to see his dad. His mum told him that she might go to prison if he didn't go. That worried him, who would look after him then. His brother Terry went one day to see Dad but he was sick in the car of the lady who took him. She brought him home. "Your Dad goes to the contact centre every week just to wait for you," the lady told him. He could wait all he liked, he wasn't going anywhere near him soon.

## Six

After she gave birth to her the midwife plonked her straight on her chest, "Here we are mummy, now give her a good feed," the midwife had said. "Sit up a bit and I'll help you," but it hadn't worked. The midwife had taken her away, wrapped her in a blue blanket and put her in a see through cot next to her bed. Melissa hadn't cried, she was a good baby, everyone said that. Bottle feeding went well but she knew that something wasn't quite right between her and Melissa, she didn't really want to look after her. She took her back to the flat and the health visitor said she was doing very well. Once or twice Gary came by to see her, he gave her some money, it was very handy. He peeped in at the cot, "she is well cute," he said, "well cute." "Not so cute at two in the morning," said Amy, you should be here then. "You know I can't be," said Gary and turned on his heel and left.

In a year a lot had happened. The old lady next door had complained to the social that she cried all the time, Melissa never stopped, that was true. She now had a social worker and someone came every day to check on the baby, she knew that they were worried that she might have hit her, they had once thought they had seen bruises on Melissa. Now they were talking about maybe her going to live with foster parents. "Who is the baby's father?" asked the social worker. "Gary," she said. She actually couldn't remember his last name and this made her feel funny. She knew where he lived with his wife and two children and she gave them his address. At the end of the Court hearing the Judge said that she could look after Melissa providing she had some help but that Gary would see Melissa every fortnight.

Here she was on a Saturday morning waiting outside with all the other mothers, with all the other dads, with all the other buggies, with all the other kids inside and hanging on to them. She was surprised that he turned up. "All right, mate," he said. "No, I'm not all right," said Amy, "and I'm not your mate, so wrong on both accounts, Gary." She handed him Melissa and walked off.

At the Contact Centre Gary tried hard with Melissa, he walked round with her, he got out toys that made a noise but Melissa would just cry and had her arms out towards the door, the one her mother had walked through. He didn't know what to do.

## Seven

He felt stupid buying Easter eggs in January but he would only be seeing his son four times a year, that's what had been agreed, so here he was with two carrier bags, some Christmas presents, some Easter eggs and some clothes that his mother thought that the boy might like. He had been very pleased to marry Donna, he knew that she had only done it for the money so that he could get his immigration status but he had been very grateful. Neither of them had bargained for the fact that they actually ended up quite liking each other. Between them they had produced little Jackie. She made it clear that she wouldn't stay with him. "I don't actually love you," Donna had said, "you knew that right from the start, I never pretended." "In my country sons are special, we don't just walk away from our children," he'd said. She hadn't listened. "If you want to see him you'll have to go through the Courts, I don't think it's right, I'm moving on in my life and I don't want you involved, I told you that, I told you right from the start."

The story had been told to the Judge. He understood that Donna was moving abroad, he understood how the couple had come to marry. What was more confusing was how little Jackie had come to be born when Donna had said that she had never liked him. That hadn't made sense but then not everything did, it was ordered that he should have contact with his son four times a year.

Now as he waited he realised a whole hour of the two hours had gone by and no-one had come, she had not kept her promise and he felt stupid sitting there with all the bags. He went up to the lady in her office, "I don't think they are coming," she said, "would you like me to call someone for you?" He hadn't got a number for her. "I don't think so," he said, "I don't have her details." "Maybe you'll have to go back to Court," she told him. "Maybe I just can't bring myself to do it, I've got some Easter eggs in here and some clothes my mum sent over, give them to someone you think might need them," he said as he left.

## Eight

When Sonny came back from seeing his mum it was always difficult, he couldn't get a word out of him. He and Dawn learnt it was best to let him come round in his own time. Sometimes he'd make the mistake when he picked him up, he'd ask, "how's your mum?" He knew how Ellie was, he knew from looking at her from afar how much weight she'd lost, how agitated she was, her lank hair and her permanently ringing hands. "She's fine,"

Sonny would say, "She's really good, she's starting a new job next week." Once Dawn had found in his bedroom an advert that he'd drafted for the local newspaper; he was selling his electronic toys, he knew why, to give Ellie money. He knew that Sonny stole from him and gave Ellie his findings. He didn't mind, he would give Ellie money if she really needed it, but he knew exactly where it would go and perhaps Sonny also knew that Ellie would immediately spend anything she had on drugs.

One day when Sonny came back from the Contact Centre he was behaving very oddly. He'd run straight up into his bedroom and didn't come out for a couple of hours. He shouted up the stairs, "You all right, Sonny?" There was no reply. He went into his room. Sonny was asleep but he couldn't wake him up. Dawn came running up, "We need an ambulance."

When his stomach had been pumped out they found that he'd taken heroin. It had almost killed Sonny. He knew where it had come from and that he would never forgive Ellie. When Sonny could speak he said, "I'm sorry, Dad, I found it in her bag and thought if I took it that she wouldn't have to."

## Stunned by the Misery

Across the Rectory Road car park a mother screams at her child in the pushchair she is steering with one hand, while the other hand drags a lurching, sobbing toddler wearing an all-in-one suit. "Hold up that f…..g balloon will you," she says to the infant in the pushchair. The orange balloon on a stick has come close to the ground and the child responds by lifting it higher. The group go past me, cars back into spaces, it's raining, it's murky, people are running to the pay machines, their heads bent.

There is a sudden bang and then silence before a woman's voice screams out, "Now you've burst it, that's the end of that you little shit. Serves you right, it's gone forever." The toddler, in fright, runs across the car park under the wheels of a reversing car.

That evening when she walked back through the park it was busy, the sound of the ring road was like an engine, continually in the background. A man sat on the park bench resting on his knees, wearing shorts, reading the newspaper; he was bald and looked a bit like her dad, or how she imagined he might be. He was wearing trainers and an old England shirt was round his waist; the man looked at his shoes in a distracted sort of way, away from the paper. Now and again he folded it up and put it down on the seat next to him and occasionally rubbed his eyes. A group of schoolgirls were sitting in the shade. She didn't know any of them and there seemed to be a lot of them. Sometimes she would have been scared that she might be hit on by them but today she just sat down on the grass. The man on the bench got up and walked past her, she noticed that he had very white trainers and that his feet were flat, he had tattoos on his arm that she couldn't read. People had told her that she looked like her mum, she couldn't see it herself, certainly she didn't know her dad so she couldn't see any of that. Often she had wondered about him but being pregnant now things made her wonder differently. Who would the baby look like? Would he or she look like Darren? Could that be changed now? Was it set in stone for ever like most things were? Sooner or later she'd have to tell her mum, sooner or later they'd have to tell Darren's mum and dad, sooner rather than later she knew that Darren would leave her. She wanted Darren more than she wanted the baby. That was the hardest part. The baby was a link to him but with the baby he would be gone, without the baby he might stay. She got up and walked back around the side of the park past the plants with the big sticky out leaves, she liked them, they looked like her Nan's cactus, the ones they were supposed never to have touched. She remembered when she did touch them and the tiny thorns had been in her fingers for weeks, but she never told anybody because she knew what her mum would say, "you were told not to touch them, now look, you never listen, you're like your dad, he never listened either." What would her mum say now about the baby?

She walked back again up the high street and into New Look. Her friend Maeve sometimes worked there. She walked round the shop looking out for Maeve with beautiful pink hair. Maeve always seemed to know about everything but she wasn't there today or at least she couldn't find her. Wherever she looked there were women with children looking worn out, worn down, dragging children along by the hand with another in a pushchair, babies screaming for a feed, sometimes there were grandmas with babies, or were they just mums looking old. She passed Timpson's, the shoe-repairers, they seemed to be selling Christening gifts; *when did shoe repairers sell christening gifts, from now* she thought. Just as she reached Wilkinson's a voice shouted out, "Hi ye." It was Maeve. She looked beautiful as always. Her pink and gold hair hung down her back, she was wearing little white shoes and a very short skirt and a brilliant blue lacy top. "Hi ye," she said, "didn't you hear me?" "I just went into New Look to see if you were there." "I'm on my lunch," said Maeve. "You all right, you want to come with me, I'm just going shopping for my mum in Wilkinson's." "Yeh, all right" she said. She picked up a wire basket and Maeve headed determinedly for the tampon section. She picked up six packets of Night Time Extra. "My mum's in the change," said Maeve, "she has blood everywhere, I don't know what to do to help." "Oh," she said, "Anyway, I need to buy a card for my nephew," said Maeve, and they went off to look at the birthday cards. They came away with a Fireman Sam I Am Two. Maeve said, "He's real cute, I wouldn't mind if he were mine." "Wouldn't you," she said, "wouldn't you really." "No, he's real cute, I look after him quite a bit," said Maeve. "Anyway what you doing down town?" She couldn't answer, she didn't know what to say. "I just wasn't in work today," she said. "Are you sick," said Maeve, "you look sort of odd." "I'm not sick I've just got a lot to think about." "Oh, yeh," said Maeve, "would that be Darren you've got to think about." "That and a few other things," she said, "I wouldn't waste time thinking about Darren," said Maeve, "what is there to think about with Darren, it wouldn't take you long to think about him." Maeve didn't have a regular boyfriend although she could have had anyone she liked, she just couldn't be bothered, it seemed. She liked having fun too much. She always seemed to be busy with other things, things to do with her family. There were a lot of them, Maeve had three brothers and an older sister, they often did things together. She was jealous. It would good to be part of a big family she thought. Maeve said, "Gotta go back to work now, anyway, what you doing tonight?" "Er, not sure," she said. "I'm going to be down the town," said Maeve. "I might see you then." "Yes, see you," she said and walked off.

Waiting for the bus she started to feel a bit faint. She leant against the plastic edge of the bus stop seat and luckily the bus came along a few minutes later. Just before she boarded the bus a woman was running along the pavement carrying a lot of bags. It was her mum's friend Janine. She was red, puffed out, overweight, she thought she looked quite grim. She plonked herself on the seat nearest the doorway. She nodded in acknowledgement. "That was a close one," the woman said, "my feet are killing me. It's this heat, everything swells up don't it, everything's like some heaving lump. How's your mum?" she said. "Oh, she's fine," she said unconvincingly. In fact when she thought about it she didn't really know how her mum was, it seemed ages since she'd even asked her mum or thought about how she was. At the moment she couldn't think of anything but herself and what was inevitably growing inside of her.

Janine opened a packet of chocolate éclairs, "want a sweet?" she said. "Yes please." She took it gladly, she remembered that she hadn't eaten anything all day. "You don't look too right to me, you okay." "Oh, yeh," she said. "Help me off with this lot." She helped Janine off with the shopping, there was a lot of clanking as she realised that she had at least two bottles of wine and a bottle of whisky in one of the bags; no wonder it was heavy. There was also a 2lb bag of potatoes in the other bag and a huge packet of toilet rolls. She thought about Janine stuffing her face with potatoes and swilling it down with the scotch and the wine and sitting on the toilet many minutes later. That's disgusting she thought, that's quite disgusting. There was a mess in Janine's garden as they walked up to the front door, it was everywhere, there were old milk cartons, bits of cars, a derelict caravan in the driveway that you had to squeeze past to get to the front door. Janine lived here on her own with her three children. The boys were a handful, they were very grim, nobody liked them, except for some reason her mum liked Janine. She thought maybe they'd gone to school together, she'd forgotten now. She dropped the bags on the step, "Thanks love," she said, "tell your mum I was asking after her." She made her way back down the path and stepped in a lot of chewing gum which made a mess of her sandals. It would take her ages to get that off.

# The Seat

1.

She tells me that she is sitting here because she has recently stopped work, that she is having a baby in four weeks' time and that her home in Singleton is north facing. The flat has poor light, there is no sunshine, balcony or a patio and she says that she craves the sun. Her partner is also from Albania and she tells me that he has just started, last week, with his own business cleaning cars inside and out in a car park at the back of Tesco's. They want to move but he is worried that he will not make any money. She is going back to work when the baby is three months old and her mum will then look after the child. She tells me, *that's what grandmas do, they look after the children.* She asked me what I do for work and I tell her. She says, *I don't know how anyone could harm a child but then I suppose I do. I was four when we left Yugoslavia and I saw a lot of things that made me think, I also saw my father shave off my sister's hair because she said that she loved a boy. Then we went to live in Germany and I loved it, the weather was so good, I swam every day. Now we can't go back, it's so expensive, my partner is going back next week. Do you think he will come back for me and the baby?*

2.

He told me that he thought he had felt dizzy and was sitting down just to catch his breath, he thought he would be all right in a minute or two. His fingers were stained with nicotine and I saw that his face was not so old. He told me that he had lived on his own now for 12 years, that his wife had died young. *Too young. She had a heart attack at 35, too much floor scrubbing on top of having the four little'uns, I reckon, but they never said.* He said that he had had a girlfriend but they had never lived together, *things are better when you know what's happening, I know what's happening if I live on my own.* He took out a cigarette. *I would offer you love, but I'm saving, saving up for a rainy day so I can blow it all at once if you know what I mean.*

*I had pigeons once upon a time, they were classy. I won prizes. Now the only prize I'll win is £10 on the lottery.*

He gets to stand up and then falls back down again, *I'm not so well as I thought.* A middle-aged woman comes by pushing a trolley. *You chatting the girls up again Brian, Millie's at home waiting for you.* The woman turns to me, *he's had four wives, they've all died young, must be what he puts in their tea.*

3.

On Monday I was looking out of the window from my office and by the seat a man was being arrested. Three police officers and the man's friend surrounded him while he was handcuffed and his pockets were searched. The contents of his pockets were removed by the police officers who were wearing plastic gloves. The man was swaying from side to side and he seemed drunk, his friend stood by with one leg against the wall with his hands in his pockets, he was moving about in a restless way. The man kept repeatedly shouting out, *Do you know what I mean?* No one seemed to know what he did mean. The police officer spoke to someone on the radio. The handcuffed man was wearing a red jacket, trousers with a big long sign up the side of one leg. The lady from the shop put out some large old plastic sweet jars with a sign saying, *free for anyone to take.* The contents of the man's pockets were all over the wet ground—a comb, a sweet, a pen, a tissue, a plastic dog and a mobile phone. The man was taken by one policeman, handcuffed, to the police car, he continued to shout out louder, *Do you know what I mean?* The remaining police officer put the contents of the man's belongings into a plastic bag. The woman from the sweet shop shouted out after them, *Ashford scum, all of you.* She looked up and saw me watching and shook her fists.

IV

# My Mother, Part 1

My mother was always in a hurry, everything she did was at double speed and with a unique and unforgettable style. An example of this was upon coming home from school one day I found that she had painted everything in the kitchen with Household brown paint. My mother liked change and got bored quickly and so on this occasion painting everything in the kitchen including the large American second-hand fridge, in Household brown paint certainly gave it a new look but rendered the boiler unusable for some time until the paint had burnt off it. The budgie, who sat on top of the fridge was saved from the transformation. Household paint was made by Woolworths, enough said.

My abiding recollection is of running next to my mother as a child and later as an adolescent as her walking speed was so fast, keeping up with her was a task of its own. On reflection, I can see that moving quickly got you out of danger. My mother had endured the London Blitz as a child and often slept in the underground stations near Crouch End, the damage to North London had been terrible and were still seen when we visited my Grandfather in Drylands Road. Mother's favourite phrase to me was "Buck up, Elaine"; I have been doing that for over 65 years now.

My parents started married life in Hilly Fields near Catford, My birth at the Charing Cross Hospital in WC1 was reportedly accompanied by the sounds of Ava Gardner in *Showboat* which was playing next to the hospital. My parents could not afford the rent in Hilly Fields and so moved to Drylands Road to live with my grandfather for a while until finances improved.

In 1953 we moved to Southall, Middlesex at 156 North Road. This was so my mother could be near to my grandmother who had divorced my grandfather some weeks before my birth. My grandmother had become a housekeeper to an extraordinary man, Charles Tordiff, an inventor of many electrical devices including the wire recorder, a prototype of the tape recorder. The house, in Morland Gardens, was a haven with sunken garden and huge greenhouses where I played with my grandmother's button box. She had been a tailor and dressmaker having made the fleecy lining of airmen's boots in the war and the red velvet cape of a notorious hunchbacked woman. The task was said to have nearly killed her, getting the hunch covered properly. My first school blazer was handmade by my grandmother and while lovingly made, including the embroidered school badge, it did not look anything like the ones the other children wore, but off I went wearing it without understanding the implications. At that time, Southall was becoming a significant Sikh capital. To me this was fascinating as the landscape changed and shops became emporiums of different encounters. Shortly before leaving the area we were one of the only white families in North Road.

My first school, Dormers Wells was short lived as we moved not long after. I didn't mind it much and my dislike of school and education generally came later. Two things amazed and astonished me at the age of five; one was when a little boy was asked to go to the front by our teacher and was slapped on the back of his legs very hard and for about four minutes with a ruler. We were told that the same would happen to us if we did not do as we were told. I remember the face of the little boy even now, his red raw legs and face in a knot. The second thing which astonished to me was the sight of my friend, Yvonne Fletcher, who was allowed to sit on the back in her own little seat on her mother's bicycle. My parents, my mother in particular, had a firm and clear anxiety about bikes and I was always told that I would never be allowed a bicycle, so the idea of an adult who allowed their child to sit in this very wonderful position on the back was remarkable. Going home to tea with Yvonne Fletcher one afternoon her mother perched me on the back of the bike under my mother's strict instructions that I must only be wheeled along the pavement so the thrill was not quite the same, but doubtless safer.

When I was six years old my parents moved to Lee Green in South London at 71 Horn Park Lane. This move again was made by following my grandmother who moved to Exford Road in Grove Park This was for us a far better and more gracious house, semi-detached but with a long garden with a pond. I was to attend the Horn Park Lane School which I walked to every day; this involved crossing the busy A20 of Westbourne Avenue and then going up through the council estate until the school was reached. Often I would go with other children, my friend Jennifer White who lived across the road or with Keith Bloomfield, a little lad who had started his journey from the bottom of Upwood Road. He must have left very early; he was only six and, being fascinated by all insects and leaves, his journey to school would take him twice as long as everyone else as he inevitably had one foot in the gutter and the other in the hedge.

Growing up in Horn Park Lane was interesting. My friend Jennifer White across the road had the kind of lifestyle that I longed for; not only had she attended the independent Riverstone School for a while, it was also planned that she would attend Blackheath High School, another independent school, when she was 11. Jennifer had ballet lessons, something I always longed for. My mother was an inveterate jumble-sale person and together we would visit every church hall where such an event was being held. On one occasion I found some second-hand ballet shoes; I was in seventh heaven, they were maroon, they were also an adult size 4 and I was a child's size 10. This didn't deter me and with elastic bands and cardboard at the back I wore them all over the house. Jennifer White asked why I was wearing them and I told her that I too was having ballet lessons. She informed me that they were the wrong size, but that didn't matter to me, it was a lie but I was now a contender. Jennifer's father was a photographer on the *Daily Sketch* and the envy of Jennifer White was further enhanced as years later she had tickets for *Top of the Pops* and her father took photos of The Beatles. I couldn't compete with that, as by then my social life was at the Methodist Church Hall in Burnt Ash Lane. My father ran the Sunday School, a continuous sore point with my mother who loathed the church, having been raised in a Salvation Army background. Her life and interest was film, film stars, notorious criminal trials and crooks, a passion which remained with her until the end. I remember well the look of the Sunday School leaders when my prize for good attendance, chosen by my mother, was *Film Show Annual*.

When I was eight my mother became depressed. This was very frightening and marked the start of my anxieties over going to school and leaving her at home. Once or twice I walked home from school during the day to check she was all right. When my mother had her nervous breakdown, a familiar turn of phrase in those times, I thought the world had ended; she became very thin and her hair started to fall out. She had always looked smart and fashion had been a great thing for her, albeit that my grandmother still made many of our clothes. Mum became afraid of going out, agoraphobic, she wasn't sure what she was afraid of but knew she didn't want to leave the house.

My father went to prayer meetings and they prayed for my mother's health. This made her worse and she particularly hated the Methodist vicar who, I well recall once gave a sermon on the perils of young men who wore elastic-sided boots. He was Welsh and emphasized the gravity of this depravity with his sonorous tones. It took years for my mother to recover but not before her problems were identified as being linked with an acute thyroid disorder.

My mother's sense of humour was legendary and remained so despite her illness, something she had inherited from her father who always had the funniest slant on the world. Their habit of talking to everybody and anybody who stood next to them for more than a second has continued as a family characteristic.

My mother's warm and humane style continued throughout her life but she her fear of being alone remained. My grandmother had a Victorian interest in death and the afterlife which predominated; she was a Medium and had been a famous speaker in the 1930s. My mother would say that she was fed up with hearing about death, that life was for the living. She would always buy flowers for herself professing loudly that they were no good to dead people.

My mother did not enjoy cooking; she was a fastidious housewife and in fact a good cook, but having people to the house worried her and was one of the sources of acrimony between my parents; that and the church. My mother worried about what she would give people to eat, about them staying too long—longer than three minutes—and importantly, making a mess. I remember once when somebody came to the house to see us, unannounced. We were in the middle of our lunch, my mother gathered up the four corners of the table cloth, complete with plates knives and forks and the contents of the meal and placed in a cupboard much to the amazement of my father and I.

Mother did things that were expedient and, in the ancient house she later shared with my father before his death, she would throw her tea-bags out of the window as it was quicker than the bin. For her it was out of sight and out of mind. As the cottage bordered the churchyard I often wonder what anyone made of the increasing amount of tea-bags accumulated over the five happy years they lived there before my father's sudden death.

My mother spoke often about her childhood in Crouch End, about enduring the war under the Morrison table shelter they had in the kitchen and her friendship with Peter Sellers who had moved to Muswell Hill in 1935, just up the road. My grandmother's origins were half Polish-Jewish, a long story in itself. One of her sisters had married an Italian who was interned during the war; she died of TB and so her son was raised with my mother. He was a sad child who later started a famous Hi-Fi shop in Hampstead. Peter Sellers brought him famous customers who all wanted Hi-Fidelity equipment.

The house in Drylands Road had four floors and during the war and indeed after it, was full of tenants. One such tenant was Miss Green who, it was strongly rumoured, was a spy. One day she just completely vanished, leaving a flat full of belongings, later removed by "some men".

When I was ten I suffered a serious accident; I went horse riding with a child of my parents' friends, the Maynards. They lived in Bexley and the stable was near to them. My anxiety about being killed outright by almost anything, particularly bicycles and horses, probably did not make me the easiest horse rider and doubtless the horse knew this. I was riding a horse called Pinky—he had a brother called Perky. The girl leading me on a lunging rope had possibly never done the job before. Pinky saw Perky and took off with me on his back. The result was serious, leaving me with a leg shattered in several places. The event bought me to one of the first of many significant events of my life: separation from my parents. As a much-loved only child, cosseted and having worn a liberty bodice from the moment I could breathe until I was sixteen, the idea of being away from my parents' influence and their tender loving care brought its own challenges. We had a family car but it didn't go well and in those days Lee Green was some distance from the West Hill Hospital in Dartford, where I was an in-patient, placed on traction. My mother would often make the journey by train, and it would take her all day. Being in traction for three months was a disturbing experience, but I was for once immobile and also a captive audience. I had no schooling for almost a year. Studying the other children around me I was amazed by their different lifestyles, their situations and how they coped with their chronic illnesses. The girl opposite to me, Monica, was almost blind. Surgeons worked hard to restore her sight but by the time Monica was discharged, having been a patient for over six months, she only had some peripheral vision. I remember Monica's visitors, her mother with dyed red hair who came to see her every three weeks with a number of different men friends whom Monica called Uncle. My eyes were opened yet further by my closest bed-mate, Rosanna, who taught me and told me all about the facts of life and her own experiences of having been sexually abused by her brother from the age of four; she never told an adult. Rosanna had unexplained chronic stomach pain which, looking back, were understandable.

I had always been a fussy eater and being in hospital my parents were worried that I would starve to death. They made sure that I didn't and my father, who had the opportunity of many delicious dinners via his work, would bring me breast of chicken and potted shrimps from the Great Eastern Hotel, a place that I believed was entirely exotic and to which I could not wait one day to be taken. My father was true to his promise and after I had recovered he took me to London and together we had lunch where the waiters were told that I was the child they had been feeding with titbits from the kitchen.

It was during this time that I resolved that I too wanted to become a doctor. The surgeon who visited me regularly was Mr Hulbert, a Consultant Orthopaedic Surgeon of great skill who, at that time, seemed to me to be a very elderly man. I was at once enthralled by the skill of doctors who could turn the lives of my hospital friends around by their expertise, I too wanted to change the world. But more of that another time; it was, after all, 1961.

# My Father, Part 1

My father, Harry, was one of six children born in Lewisham, south-east London, in May 1919. He was the middle child, having two younger sisters, a younger brother and two older brothers. At one point in the family history another boy was adopted into the family when his parents died, making them a group of seven. In common with so many of that time, the family were extremely poor, but they had a home at 13 Mercia Grove, Lewisham and, importantly, love and affection.

There is a photograph of which my father was most proud. It is of him with a small bicycle, at about seven years of age. In the foreground his sister Florrie wears a torn and tattered dress, depicting a familiar sight from those times. The picture is important because it is the only thing my father owned as a child. The bicycle was returned to the shop the following day to pay for food.

My paternal grandfather was a munitions worker at the Woolwich Arsenal but was often without work. He was involved in the hunger marches of the 1920s and joined the Jarrow Crusades in October 1936. He endured a hard life and, in common with all members of the Randell family, he died before receiving his pension. My paternal grandmother was born in Greenwich; family myth says that her father traded in diamonds, but there was no evidence of this. Florence was uneducated but I remember her always doing the crossword every time I saw her in the basement, where she sat, immovable, by the coal fire. Nanny Randell, as she was known, enjoyed a drink, something that my father particularly loathed and she was often found in the Sultan pub in Lewisham, having drunk too many pints. She had endured a hard life but managed to keep the majority of her children in close proximity. Auntie Win and Alf were at number 15, Auntie Florrie and Fred at 17 and Uncle Bob and Jean were upstairs at 13. Visiting the family was an all-day event, being entertained from one house to the other. Uncle Fred and Ivy lived in Hither Green where they chain-smoked Kensitas cigarettes, furnishing their home with goods bought with the

Kensitas coupons. The more you smoked, the more goods you could acquire. Uncle Arthur and Ann lived in Plumstead; along with ourselves, they were the out-of-towners, who lived in Lee Green. We were known as "posh" because Harry had made good and was rich. Indeed, for years, my father supported his mother financially; it was what you did.

A major part of my father's entire life was his involvement in the church. As a small boy, he joined the Sunday School and the Boys' Brigade at the local Methodist Church in Lewisham. They were his role models, and likely his main support system. Dad left school at the age of 14 and the school report of July 1933 from the Headmaster of the Hither Green LCC school describes him as having a "well-earned place at the top of the class. He will develop to be a diligent and earnest employee."

In 1934 my father found work at the Oil Well Engineering Company, in Moorgate, as an office boy. He remained working there for the following 28 years, save for the period when he was in the army. When war broke out he signed up with the Royal Engineers, which became part of the infamous Forgotten 14th Army that was in Burma to fight the Japanese. In common with those who served and survived in Burma, he spoke very little of the horrors and atrocities that he and others had endured. Enough, however, was said to give us to understand that the experiences were traumatic and the effects lifelong. When finally he was demobbed from the Army, sometime in 1945, Dad returned to his old job in Moorgate where he met my mother, Daphne, who was working as a secretary; my father was 8 years her senior. They married in 1949. Having little money, my father often walked from Hilly Fields near Catford, where they lived, to Moorgate. He was stick-thin and remained so throughout his life, since, like my mother, he never stopped moving.

In hindsight, Dad was involved in too many things. Certainly, the church used up a great deal of his energy, as did amateur dramatics and, once we had a proper home, gardening. He was a hopeless DIY man; "I'm no Barry Bucknell," he would say, as shelves were put up at angles and pictures fell regularly from the walls. Dad would encourage me to make miniature gardens in a seed box using soil, making a miniature pond from a mirror, using moss, a tiny seat from plasticine and tiny trees from twigs. It was perhaps a precursor for me for sand-tray work with troubled children.

My father adored my mother and they made a good team. He never returned from a trip abroad or even to the shops without a gift or a bunch of flowers. Dad loved socialising and having people to our home. Mum hated this as she would become anxious that people would need to eat and also that they might stay too long, that is, longer than five minutes. It was the one bone of contention between them. As a teenager, I joined the Peace Pledge Union and CND. Dad had not been a conscientious objector in the war and he enjoyed nothing better than long, heated debates with my friends, many of whom he persuaded to read Albert Schweitzer—someone he quoted often—much to my deep embarrassment at the time. "The only way out of today's misery is for people to become worthy of each other's trust." My friends loved debating with my dad and envied me that I had that possibility. Fathers in the 1950s and '60s were not always easy with their role.

To my knowledge, I disappointed my father only twice. The first time was when I truanted for two days during my first year of grammar school. I had been terrified of a French teacher, Miss Barnes, who had thrown my book across the room towards my head when she saw my homework. It had been worked on—by me—so many times in my efforts to get it right, using an ink eradicator, that holes had been worn right through the pages. I was worried about going back for more and so went with a friend to Greenwich Park instead of school. So far, so good, except I tripped while running downhill towards the museum and broke my toe. On arrival at home, the offended toe swelled and was painful. I said that I had injured myself playing lacrosse. The next day my father telephoned the school to express his concern that I had not been treated by a doctor. They of course, confirmed that I had not been in school. The balloon went up, but with good results. Miss Barnes was told to calm down. My mother confided to me her significant upset with a needlework teacher who had distressed her so much that she had smuggled her embroidery home in her knickers so my grandmother could do it instead. My father said he was disappointed that I had not been able to tell him my worries.

The second occasion was years later and was my one and only foray into the Juvenile Court as a criminal. I had evaded my train fare getting to London to meet a boyfriend who lived in Balham, and was prosecuted by the Transport Police. My dad was clearly distressed that I had possibly embarked on a life of crime. Sadly, he didn't live long enough to see the thousands of reports I have subsequently written over the years on behalf of and about children and young people in trouble, in attempts to improve their lot.

Dad had a wonderful sense of humour and was well known for being careful that no jokes or comments should ever be used against anyone. This made him popular with those who knew him; they felt they could trust him, which was unusual in the cut-throat oil industry of the 1960s. If anyone ever behaved badly or was criticised by my mother or me, he would always say, to know all is to forgive all, you have to understand why people do certain things and behave in a certain way before jumping in, Elaine. It's no wonder that social work was a career possibility. My father left the Oil Well Engineering Company to become self-employed in the late 1960s at the time of oil and gas exploration in the North Sea. He was responsible for the erection of the first fixed, concrete oil-platform; he was rightly proud, but feared the long-term impact on Scotland, a place he loved both as a walker and fisherman.

Dad in fact enjoyed and was involved in every sport he could, excelling at tennis, being well respected by the Rye Tennis Club, and was also an excellent cricketer. Our holidays were always based on rivers in the UK so that he could fish. I would have my own rod too, set up between watching my mother trying to sunbathe on the riverbank with her movie books beside her. Mum hated sport of all kinds and watching dad fish was a double purgatory.

My father's family had all their lives feared being sent to the workhouse, a reality they had doubtless narrowly avoided since, it's worth remembering, it was not until 1929 that local authorities had the responsibility to change workhouses into infirmary hospitals. The anxiety over seeking medical help was deep-seated and, despite his intelligence, dad resisted seeing a doctor when he had chest pain and so he, like all his siblings, died before his sixtieth birthday.

When he died in 1979 over 300 people wrote to my mother and me, saying how much he had affected their lives for the better. I only found it bearable to read some of the letters recently; people spoke of his kindness, his generosity, his constant and genuine interest in the welfare of others and of his diligent work, in addition to his tireless energy and, importantly, his quick sense of humour. Over £8,000 was raised in lieu of flowers at his funeral and the roof of Snargate Church on Romney Marsh, next door to where my parents lived, was replaced: a fitting tribute.

www.ingramcontent.com/pod-product-compliance
Lightning Source LLC
Chambersburg PA
CBHW031152160426
43193CB00008B/343